Anda Thomas
6/05

Slow Cooker

Pillsbury

PILLSBURY®
DOUGHBOY™

RECIPES

The
Pillsbury
Company

PILLSBURY®
DOUGHBOY™

Slow Cooker
RECIPES

140 New Ways
to Have Dinner
Ready and Waiting!

Clarkson Potter/Publishers
New York

ALSO BY PILLSBURY®

Pillsbury: Best Chicken Cookbook
Pillsbury: Best Cookies Cookbook
Pillsbury: Best Muffins & Quick Breads Cookbook
Pillsbury: Best of the Bake-Off ® Cookbook
Pillsbury: Fast and Healthy® Cookbook
Pillsbury: Best Desserts
Pillsbury: The Best of Classic® Cookbooks
Pillsbury: One-Dish Meals Cookbook
Pillsbury: Complete Cookbook
Pillsbury: 30-Minute Meals
Pillsbury Doughboy™: Family Pleasing Recipes
Pillsbury: Appetizers

For more recipes, visit www.pillsbury.com.

FRONT COVER PHOTOGRAPH: SWISS STEAK SUPPER, PAGE 21
BACK COVER PHOTOGRAPHS (FROM TOP TO BOTTOM):
ITALIAN SAUSAGE LASAGNA, PAGE 47; GRANDMA'S CHICKEN
NOODLE SOUP, PAGE 99; CHICKEN IN WINE SAUCE, PAGE 58
FRONTIS PHOTOGRAPH: BEEF AND BEAN TAMALE PIE,
PAGE 26

Published by Clarkson Potter/Publishers,
New York, New York.
Member of the Crown Publishing Group,
a division of Random House, Inc.
www.randomhouse.com

The trademarks referred to herein are trademarks of
The Pillsbury Company and its affiliates.

CLARKSON N. POTTER is a trademark and POTTER and
colophon are registered trademarks of Random House, Inc.

Printed in USA

Library of Congress Cataloging-in-Publication Data
Pillsbury Doughboy slow cooker recipes : 140 new ways to
have dinner ready and waiting! / The Pillsbury Company.—
1st ed.   p.   cm
Includes bibliographical references and index.
1. Electric cookery, slow.   I. The Pillsbury Company
TX827.P55   2003
641.5'884—dc21   2002007070

ISBN 0-609-60862-2

10   9   8   7   6   5   4   3   2   1

FIRST EDITION

CREDITS
THE PILLSBURY COMPANY
Director, Book and Web Publishing: Kim Walter
Manager, Books: Lois Tlusty
Editor: Kelly Kilen
Recipe Development and Testing: Pillsbury Test Kitchens
Photography: General Mills Photo Studios and
General Mills Image Library

CLARKSON POTTER/PUBLISHERS
THE CROWN PUBLISHING GROUP
President and Publisher: Jenny Frost
Senior Vice President/Editorial Director: Lauren Shakely
Senior Editor/Strategic Marketing Director: Katie Workman
Editorial Assistant: Lisa Nager
Creative Director: Marysarah Quinn
Designer: Caitlin Daniels Israel
Managing Editor: Amy Boorstein
Associate Managing Editor: Mark McCauslin
Senior Production Editor: Sibylle Kazeroid
Production Superviser: Linnea Knollmueller
Director of Publicity: Leigh Ann Ambrosi

contents

INTRODUCTION

Top 10 Tips for Slow Cooker Success

page 6

ONE

Meaty Main Dishes

page 10

TWO

Busy-Day Chicken and Turkey

page 54

THREE

Super Soups, Stews and Chilies

page 90

FOUR

Slow-Cooked Sandwiches

page 130

FIVE

Very Easy Vegetables and Sides

page 154

INDEX

page 172

introduction

welcome to pillsbury doughboy slow cooker recipes

As busy lives speed up, cooks are slowing down by making the most of their slow cooker. Slow cooking is great when you want to "fix it and forget it," so you can enjoy the best part of the meal—sharing it with family and friends. Check out these slow cooker secrets to help you make your recipes their slow-simmered best.

Top 10 Tips for Slow Cooker Success

1. Get to Know Your Cooker

First things first: Become familiar with your slow cooker. Just as ovens cook differently, so do slow cookers.

- Some slow cookers cook food continuously at very low wattage. This type of cooker is called a *continuous slow cooker*. The heating coils are in the outer metal shell, and they stay on constantly to heat the crockery liner. A continuous slow cooker has two or three fixed settings: low (about 200°F.), high (about 300°F.) and in some models, auto, which shifts from high to low automatically. It may or may not have a removable ceramic liner.
- Another type of slow cooker is the *intermittent cooker*, which has a heating element in the base on which the container stands. The heat cycles on and off to maintain a constant temperature. If your slow cooker has a dial with numbers or temperatures, it is an intermittent cooker. It's important to read and follow the manufacturer's instructions for these cookers so you can determine what settings to use.
- Slow cookers also come in many sizes, from 1 quart (perfect for dips and spreads) up to 6 quarts (ideal for large cuts of meats and crowd-size recipes). Check the capacity of your cooker to see if it fits the size recommended in the recipe you are making. Generally, slow cookers work most efficiently when they're between two-thirds and three-quarters full of food.

2. Begin with the Basics

Successful slow cooking starts with some simple strategies:

- Before adding food to the slow cooker, spray the inside of it with nonstick cooking spray to make cleanup easier.

- Food placed in the bottom of the slow cooker will often be moister (from being in the cooking liquid), and meat, such as ribs, roasts and chicken, will fall off the bones sooner. To help meats cook evenly, rotate meats halfway through cooking.
- Root vegetables, such as potatoes and carrots, take longer to cook, so cut them into smaller pieces and place them in the bottom of the slow cooker (closest to the heat source).
- To keep fat and calories in your finished dish to a minimum, remove the skin from poultry and trim excess fat from meats before cooking.
- Cook and drain ground meats before adding them to the slow cooker, to reduce the fat content of the finished dish.
- Brown meats and poultry in a skillet before placing them in the slow cooker. Although this isn't necessary, browning can enhance the flavor and appearance of your finished dish.

3. Time It Right

One of the great things about a slow cooker is that it needs very little clock watching. For the most part, you can prepare the recipe, turn on the cooker and then forget about it until you're ready to eat. Although slow-cooked recipes don't require any tricky timing, here are a few timely tips to keep in mind:

- Many recipes use the low setting because a longer cooking time often fits better into your daily schedule. However, you can shorten the cooking time by turning the slow cooker to high for 1 hour, which counts as 2 hours on low.
- Smaller is not always faster. Baby carrots, for example, take longer to cook than some other veggies. Don't forget to check for doneness.
- Slow cookers offer flexibility. Most cooked food can be held up to an hour on the low setting without overcooking. Some recipes, such as dips and spreads, can be kept on low for several hours. Just be sure to check occasionally to see if they need to be stirred.
- Resist the temptation to lift the lid on your slow cooker until shortly before serving. Removing the cover allows heat to escape and adds 15 to 20 minutes to the cooking time. If you want to see inside, try spinning the cover until the vapors fall off.

4. Add a Flash of Flavor

To get the most flavor from the foods you cook in your slow cooker, try these hints:

- Use dried leaf herbs instead of ground because they retain their flavor during the longer cooking time. Fresh herbs should be stirred in during the last hour of cooking so they stay flavorful. It's always a good idea to taste before serving to see if additional seasoning is needed.
- Ground red pepper (cayenne) and hot pepper sauce tend to become bitter during long slow cooking. Use small amounts and taste during the last hour of cooking to decide whether you need to add more.
- For a more pronounced flavor in soups and stews, substitute broth for the water or add bouillon cubes with the water.
- You can develop the flavors in the juices by removing the lid and cooking on the high setting for the last 20 to 30 minutes. This evaporates the water so the flavors become more concentrated and intense. Use the juices as a base for a sauce or gravy, or serve them as is over meats.

5. Plan a Perfect Ending

Sometimes you have to save the best for last, and slow cooking is no exception.

- Some herbs, such as oregano and basil, change flavor with an extended cooking time. Stir these in during the final hour of cooking.

- Fish and seafood fall apart during long hours of cooking, and some seafood, such as shrimp, becomes very tough. Add these ingredients during the last hour of cooking.
- Tender vegetables, such as fresh tomatoes, mushrooms and zucchini, should be added during the last 30 minutes so they don't become overcooked and mushy.
- Frozen vegetables will keep their bright color and crisp-tender texture if you add them during the last 30 minutes of cooking.
- Long-cooked dairy products such as milk, sour cream and cheese have a tendency to curdle. Keep sauces and gravies from "breaking down" by adding these ingredients during the last 30 minutes of cooking.
- For a little extra flavor or texture, sprinkle the top of your slow cooker meal with chopped fresh herbs, grated cheese, crushed croutons or corn chips, chopped tomatoes or sliced green onions just before serving.

6. Thicken It Up

Slow cookers are covered during cooking, so you will have an ample supply of rich, flavorful juices. Use these juices as a base for gravy or a sauce.

- To make gravy, pour the juices into a saucepan. Remove and discard any excess fat. For every cup of juice, use 1 tablespoon of cornstarch or 2 tablespoons of all-purpose flour. For a thinner sauce, decrease the cornstarch or flour by half. Mix the cornstarch or flour with a small amount of cold water, stirring well. Stir into juices and cook over medium-low heat, stirring occasionally, until mixture is smooth and bubbly.
- To thicken stews or other main dishes, turn the slow cooker to the high setting. For each 2 cups of liquid, mix 2 tablespoons cornstarch and 2 tablespoons cold water (or ¼ cup all-purpose flour and ¼ cup cold water). Stir mixture into the cooker. Cover and cook for 20 to 30 minutes.

7. Play It Safe

Be "food safe" and check this list of food safety guidelines before you use your slow cooker.

- Thaw meat and poultry in the refrigerator or in a microwave oven following the manufacturer's directions. Do not thaw at room temperature.
- Cook and drain all ground meats before adding them to the slow cooker to destroy any bacteria that the meat may contain.
- Do not undercook foods. For food-safety reasons, slow cooker recipes containing raw poultry or beef should cook a minimum of 3 hours. Do not cook whole chickens in a slow cooker because the temperature of the chicken cannot reach the desired level quickly enough for food safety.
- Don't use your slow cooker as a storage container. Remove leftovers from the slow cooker and refrigerate or freeze as soon as you are finished eating. Cooked food shouldn't stand at room temperature longer than 1 hour.
- Food should not be reheated in the slow cooker. Instead, reheat food in a saucepan on top of the stove or in the microwave.

8. Take It to Go

A slow cooker is the perfect appliance to take to potlucks, bring to family gatherings or carry to the cabin. Here are some handy tips to help you tote your food:

- Wrap the slow cooker in a towel or newspaper to keep it warm, then place it in a box (or other container) that will stay flat in your car.

- Attach rubber bands around the handles and lid to secure the lid when traveling.
- Serve cooked food within an hour, or plug in the slow cooker and set on the low (or "keep warm") setting to keep the food warm for hours.

9. Adapt Your Own Recipes

When you want to use a favorite family recipe in the slow cooker, consider these things:
- Look for a similar recipe in this cookbook to use a guide for quantities, amount of liquid and cooking time.
- Unless you are making a soup, reduce the amount of liquid in your recipe by about half because liquids do not boil away as much as in other methods of cooking.
- Use less-expensive cuts of meat, which will work well in the moist heat and low temperatures of the slow cooker. Trim as much visible fat as possible from the meat before cooking so there is less fat to remove from the finished dish.
- Instead of using fresh dairy products, such as cheese and milk, which can curdle, try canned condensed soups, nonfat milk powder or canned evaporated milk. Or add the fresh ingredients near the end of cooking.
- Be sure to allow sufficient cooking time. Most soups, stews and one-dish meals require 8 to 10 hours on the low setting.

10. Cook It Right at High Altitude

For people who live at higher altitudes (3,500 feet and above), everyday cooking, including slow cooking, presents unique challenges. Trial and error is often the best way to make improvements because no set rules apply to all recipes. Following these guidelines will help:
- Most foods take longer to cook, particularly meats cooked in boiling liquid. The time may be up to twice as long as the recipe suggests for meats to become tender. Try cooking meats on the high setting instead of on low to shorten the cooking time.
- Dried beans will also cook more slowly. We recommend using the overnight soaking in water method before cooking them in the slow cooker.
- Cutting vegetables into smaller pieces than the recipe suggests will help them cook more quickly.
- Call your local U.S. Department of Agriculture (USDA) Extension Service office, listed in the phone book under "County Government," with questions about slow cooking at high altitude.

Meet the Doughboy

Name: "Poppin' Fresh"

First Appearance: 1965

Height: 8¾ inches

Weight: 14 ounces

Eyes: Blue

Made of: Dough (what else?)

ONE
meaty main dishes

Cajun Pot Roast with Corn
and Tomatoes 12

Beef Brisket with Cranberry Gravy 13

Caramelized Onion Pot Roast 14

Mexican Round Steak 16

Saucy Pepper Steak 17

Corned Beef and Cabbage 19

Mediterranean Steak Roll 20

Swiss Steak Supper 21

Beef Ragout on Polenta 22

Burgundy Beef and Mushrooms 23

Sauerbraten 24

Rosemary Beef and Tomatoes 25

Beef and Bean Tamale Pie 26

Chili Beef and Beans 28

Picadillo with Apples and Almonds 29

Beefy Tortilla Casserole 30

Cheesy Italian Tortellini 31

Veal Paprika 32

Honey-Dijon Pork Roast 33

Porketta with Two Potatoes 34

Cranberry-Orange Pork Roast 35

Autumn Pork Roast Dinner 36

Pork and Pineapple 37

Easy Pork Chop Suey 38

Pork Chops with Spiced
Fruit Stuffing 39

Pizza Pork Chops 40

Pork Ribs with Molasses-Mustard
Sauce 41

Slow-and-Easy Barbecued Ribs 42

Key West Ribs 43

Bolognese Pasta Sauce with
Spaghetti 44

Ravioli with Smoked Sausage
and Peppers 45

Italian Sausage Lasagna 47

Scalloped Potatoes, Tomatoes
and Ham 48

Ham and Chicken Enchilada
Casserole 49

Winter Root and Sausage Casserole 50

Moroccan Lamb and Rice 51

Lamb Dijon 52

Beans 'n Wieners 53

cajun pot roast
with corn and tomatoes

YIELD: 6 SERVINGS
Prep Time: 10 minutes (Ready in 10 hours 10 minutes)

1 (2- to 2½-lb.) boneless beef chuck roast

1 tablespoon dried Cajun seasoning

1 (9-oz.) pkg. frozen corn in a pouch

½ cup chopped onion

½ cup chopped green bell pepper

1 (14.5-oz.) can diced tomatoes, undrained

⅛ teaspoon pepper

½ teaspoon hot pepper sauce

1. Rub entire surface of beef roast with Cajun seasoning. Place beef in 4- to 6-quart slow cooker. Top with corn, onion and bell pepper.

2. In small bowl, combine all remaining ingredients; mix well. Pour over vegetables and beef.

3. Cover; cook on low setting for 8 to 10 hours.

4. Remove beef from slow cooker. Cut beef into slices. Serve corn mixture with slotted spoon.

NUTRITION INFORMATION PER SERVING: Serving Size: ⅙ of Recipe • Calories 270 • Calories from Fat 80 • % Daily Value: Total Fat 9g 14% • Saturated Fat 3g 15% • Cholesterol 105mg 35% • Sodium 580mg 24% • Total Carbohydrate 12g 4% • Dietary Fiber 2g 8% • Sugars 4g • Protein 36g • Vitamin A 10% • Vitamin C 20% • Calcium 4% • Iron 25% • **DIETARY EXCHANGES:** 1 Starch, 4 Very Lean Meat, 1 Fat **OR** 1 Carbohydrate, 4 Very Lean Meat, 1 Fat

SERVE WITH
For a true Cajun-style dinner, serve hush puppies and hot cooked rice with this spicy roast. Cool down with a pitcher of iced tea, and for dessert offer up some warm bread pudding.

beef brisket
with cranberry gravy

YIELD: 8 SERVINGS

Prep Time: 10 minutes (Ready in 10 hours 10 minutes)

1 (2½-lb.) fresh beef brisket (not corned beef)

½ teaspoon salt

¼ teaspoon pepper

1 (16-oz.) can whole berry cranberry sauce

1 (8-oz.) can tomato sauce

½ cup chopped onion

1 tablespoon prepared mustard

1. Rub surface of beef brisket with salt and pepper. Place beef in 4- to 6-quart slow cooker. In small bowl, combine all remaining ingredients; mix well. Pour over beef.

2. Cover; cook on low setting for 8 to 10 hours.

3. Remove beef from slow cooker. Cut beef across grain into thin slices. If desired, skim fat from cranberry sauce in slow cooker. Serve beef with sauce.

NUTRITION INFORMATION PER SERVING: Serving Size: ⅛ of Recipe • Calories 305 • Calories from Fat 90 • % Daily Value: Total Fat 10g 15% • Saturated Fat 4g 20% • Cholesterol 80mg 27% • Sodium 440mg 18% • Total Carbohydrate 26g 9% • Dietary Fiber 2g 8% • Sugars 22g • Protein 30g • Vitamin A 6% • Vitamin C 4% • Calcium 2% • Iron 16% • **DIETARY EXCHANGES:** 1½ Fruit, 1 Vegetable, 4 Very Lean Meat, 1 Fat **OR** 1½ Carbohydrate, 1 Vegetable, 4 Very Lean Meat, 1 Fat

DOUGHBOY TIP
Whole berry cranberry sauce looks especially pretty in this dish, but you can also use a can of jellied cranberries with equally delicious results.

caramelized onion pot roast

Prep Time: 25 minutes (Ready in 10 hours 25 minutes)

1 tablespoon olive or vegetable oil

1 (4-lb.) boneless beef chuck roast

1 teaspoon salt

$1/2$ teaspoon pepper

6 medium onions, sliced

$1^1/_2$ cups beef broth

$3/4$ cup beer or nonalcoholic beer

2 tablespoons brown sugar

3 tablespoons Dijon mustard

2 tablespoons cider vinegar

1. Heat oil in large skillet over medium-high heat until hot. Add beef roast; cook about 10 minutes or until browned on all sides, turning occasionally. Sprinkle with salt and pepper.

2. Place onions in $3^1/_2$- to 6-quart slow cooker. Place beef on onions. In small bowl, combine all remaining ingredients; mix well. Pour over beef and onions.

3. Cover; cook on low setting for 8 to 10 hours.

4. With slotted spoon, remove beef and onions from slow cooker. Cut beef into slices. If desired, skim fat from beef juices in slow cooker. Serve beef with juices.

NUTRITION INFORMATION PER SERVING: Serving Size: $1/_{12}$ of Recipe • Calories 330 • Calories from Fat 170 • % Daily Value: Total Fat 19g 29% • Saturated Fat 7g 35% • Cholesterol 95mg 32% • Sodium 500mg 21% • Total Carbohydrate 9g 3% • Dietary Fiber 1g 4% • Sugars 7g • Protein 32g • Vitamin A 4% • Vitamin C 2% • Calcium 2% • Iron 20% • **DIETARY EXCHANGES:** $1/2$ Starch, 2 Vegetable, $4^1/_2$ Lean Meat, 1 Fat **OR** $1/2$ Carbohydrate, 2 Vegetable, $4^1/_2$ Lean Meat, 1 Fat

SERVE WITH

Treat your family to the ultimate comfort-food meal with this old-fashioned pot roast that has a slightly new twist. Add a side of steamed green beans and plenty of fluffy mashed potatoes to soak up all of the wonderful juices.

mexican round steak

YIELD: 6 SERVINGS

Prep Time: 15 minutes (Ready in 9 hours 15 minutes)

1½ lb. boneless beef round steak, trimmed of fat, cut into 6 serving pieces

1 cup chopped fresh cilantro

1 cup frozen whole kernel corn, thawed

3 medium stalks celery, thinly sliced (1½ cups)

1 large onion, sliced

½ cup beef broth

1 (20-oz.) jar chunky-style salsa

1 (15-oz.) can black beans, drained, rinsed

4 oz. (1 cup) shredded hot pepper Monterey Jack cheese

1. Place beef in 3½- to 6-quart slow cooker. In medium bowl, combine all remaining ingredients except cheese; mix well. Pour over beef.

2. Cover; cook on low setting for 8 to 9 hours. Sprinkle individual servings with cheese.

NUTRITION INFORMATION PER SERVING: Serving Size: ⅙ of Recipe • Calories 335 • Calories from Fat 90 • % Daily Value: Total Fat 10g 15% • Saturated Fat 5g 25% • Cholesterol 80mg 27% • Sodium 950mg 40% • Total Carbohydrate 33g 11% • Dietary Fiber 8g 32% • Sugars 7g • Protein 36g • Vitamin A 30% • Vitamin C 16% • Calcium 24% • Iron 28% • **DIETARY EXCHANGES:** 2 Starch, 1 Vegetable, 4 Very Lean Meat **OR** 2 Carbohydrate, 1 Vegetable, 4 Very Lean Meat

MAKE IT SPECIAL

Punch up the flavor in this south-of-the-border favorite by adding extra salsa and chopped fresh cilantro just before serving.

saucy pepper steak

YIELD: 6 SERVINGS

Prep Time: 20 minutes (Ready in 9 hours 35 minutes)

1½ lb. boneless beef round steak, trimmed of fat, cut into 6 serving pieces

2 medium onions, cut into ¼-inch slices

1 garlic clove, minced

½ teaspoon grated gingerroot or ¼ teaspoon ginger

1 cup beef broth

3 tablespoons soy sauce

¼ cup cold water

2 tablespoons cornstarch

2 medium green bell peppers, cut into ¾-inch strips

2 medium tomatoes, each cut into 8 wedges

1. Spray 12-inch skillet with nonstick cooking spray. Heat over medium-high heat until hot. Add beef; cook about 8 minutes or until browned, turning once.

2. Layer beef, onions, garlic and gingerroot in 3½- to 6-quart slow cooker. In small bowl, combine broth and soy sauce; mix well. Pour over beef.

3. Cover; cook on low setting for 7 to 9 hours.

4. About 15 minutes before serving, in small bowl, blend water and cornstarch until smooth. Gradually stir into beef mixture. Stir in bell peppers. Increase heat setting to high; cover and cook an additional 10 to 12 minutes or until slightly thickened. Add tomatoes; cover and cook an additional 3 minutes or just until tomatoes are thoroughly heated.

NUTRITION INFORMATION PER SERVING: Serving Size: ⅙ of Recipe • Calories 170 • Calories from Fat 35 • % Daily Value: Total Fat 4g 6% • Saturated Fat 1g 5% • Cholesterol 60mg 20% • Sodium 680mg 28% • Total Carbohydrate 11g 4% • Dietary Fiber 2g 8% • Sugars 4g • Protein 25g • Vitamin A 10% • Vitamin C 38% • Calcium 2% • Iron 14% • **DIETARY EXCHANGES:** 2 Vegetable, 3 Very Lean Meat

SERVE WITH

As colorful as it is flavorful, this saucy dish is wonderful served over a mound of hot cooked noodles or rice. Bake up a loaf of refrigerated crusty French bread, pour a tall glass of iced tea and you're ready to sit down for dinner.

corned beef and cabbage

YIELD: 8 SERVINGS

Prep Time: 15 minutes (Ready in 12 hours 50 minutes)

4 medium red potatoes, cut into 1-inch pieces

4 medium carrots, cut into 1-inch pieces

1 medium onion, cut into 6 wedges

1 (2- to 2½-lb.) corned beef brisket with seasoning packet

1 (12-oz.) can beer or nonalcoholic beer

Water

8 thin wedges cabbage

¼ cup applesauce

2 tablespoons Dijon mustard

1. In 4- to 6-quart slow cooker, combine potatoes, carrots and onion. Top with corned beef brisket; sprinkle with seasonings from packet. Add beer and enough water to just cover corned beef.

2. Cover; cook on low setting for 10 to 12 hours.

3. About 35 minutes before serving, remove corned beef from slow cooker; cover with foil. Add cabbage wedges to vegetables and broth. Increase heat setting to high; cover and cook an additional 30 to 35 minutes or until cabbage is crisp-tender.

4. Meanwhile, in small bowl, combine applesauce and mustard; mix well.

5. To serve, cut corned beef across grain into thin slices. With slotted spoon, remove vegetables from slow cooker. If desired, skim fat from juices in slow cooker. Serve vegetables with juices and corned beef with applesauce-mustard mixture.

NUTRITION INFORMATION PER SERVING: Serving Size: ⅛ of Recipe • Calories 370 • Calories from Fat 180 • % Daily Value: Total Fat 20g 31% • Saturated Fat 6g 30% • Cholesterol 100mg 33% • Sodium 1260mg 53% • Total Carbohydrate 25g 8% • Dietary Fiber 4g 16% • Sugars 7g • Protein 21g • Vitamin A 200% • Vitamin C 35% • Calcium 6% • Iron 20% • **DIETARY EXCHANGES:** 1½ Starch, 2½ Medium-Fat Meat, 1½ Fat **OR** 1½ Carbohydrate, 2½ Medium-Fat Meat, 1½ Fat

DOUGHBOY TIP

Most corned beef comes packaged with seasonings that you can use to flavor this recipe. If your corned beef doesn't have its own seasoning packet, use ½ teaspoon of black peppercorns, 6 whole cloves and 1 bay leaf.

mediterranean steak roll

YIELD: 6 SERVINGS

Prep Time: 20 minutes (Ready in 6 hours 30 minutes)

1½ lb. boneless beef top round steak
(1 inch thick), trimmed of fat

½ small onion, sliced

⅓ cup chopped green bell pepper

¼ cup chopped dry sun-dried tomatoes

1 garlic clove, minced

½ teaspoon dried oregano leaves

1 (12-oz.) jar beef gravy

¼ cup dry red wine or nonalcoholic red wine

¼ teaspoon pepper

3 tablespoons water

2 tablespoons all-purpose flour

Chopped fresh basil, if desired

1. Cut steak in half horizontally, cutting almost but not completely through one long side; open steak to make 1 large ½-inch-thick piece. If necessary, pound steak gently to make of even thickness.

2. Arrange onion, bell pepper, tomatoes, garlic and oregano evenly over steak, leaving 1 inch at one narrow end free of vegetables. Starting with other narrow end and rolling toward end free of vegetables, roll up steak. Fasten with toothpicks or secure with string.

3. Place steak roll in 4- to 6-quart slow cooker. In medium bowl, combine gravy, wine and pepper; mix well. Pour over steak roll.

4. Cover; cook on low setting for 4 to 6 hours.

5. About 10 minutes before serving, remove steak roll from slow cooker; place on serving platter. Cover with foil. In small bowl, blend water and flour until smooth. Stir into juices in slow cooker. Increase heat setting to high; cover and cook an additional 10 minutes or until thickened. Cut steak roll into slices; sprinkle with basil. Serve steak roll slices with gravy mixture.

NUTRITION INFORMATION PER SERVING: Serving Size: ⅙ of Recipe • Calories 180 • Calories from Fat 45 • % Daily Value: Total Fat 5g 8% • Saturated Fat 2g 10% • Cholesterol 60mg 20% • Sodium 390mg 16% • Total Carbohydrate 7g 2% • Dietary Fiber 1g 4% • Sugars 1g • Protein 26g • Vitamin A 0% • Vitamin C 8% • Calcium 0% • Iron 15% • **DIETARY EXCHANGES:** ½ Starch, 3½ Very Lean Meat, ½ Fat **OR** ½ Carbohydrate, 3½ Very Lean Meat, ½ Fat

DOUGHBOY TIP

Be sure to use dry sun-dried tomatoes instead of the oil-packed variety. The dried tomatoes soak up the juices and become tender during cooking. Look for them in the produce department of your supermarket near the other dried foods.

swiss steak supper

YIELD: 6 SERVINGS

Prep Time: 15 minutes (Ready in 9 hours 15 minutes)

1½ lb. boneless beef round steak (about ¾ inch thick), trimmed of fat,
cut into 6 serving pieces

½ teaspoon peppered seasoned salt

6 to 8 small red potatoes (about 1¼ lb.), cut into quarters

1½ cups fresh baby carrots

1 medium onion, sliced

1 (14.5-oz.) can diced tomatoes with basil, garlic and oregano, undrained

1 (12-oz.) jar beef gravy

1. Spray 12-inch skillet with nonstick cooking spray. Heat over medium-high heat until hot. Sprinkle beef with seasoned salt; add to skillet. Cook about 8 minutes or until browned, turning once.

2. Layer potatoes, carrots, beef and onion in 3½- to 6-quart slow cooker. In small bowl, combine tomatoes and gravy; mix well. Spoon over beef and vegetables.

3. Cover; cook on low setting for 7 to 9 hours.

NUTRITION INFORMATION PER SERVING: Serving Size: ⅙ of Recipe • Calories 235 • Calories from Fat 45 • % Daily Value: Total Fat 5g 8% • Saturated Fat 2g 10% • Cholesterol 60mg 20% • Sodium 600mg 25% • Total Carbohydrate 25g 8% • Dietary Fiber 4g 16% • Sugars 5g • Protein 27g • Vitamin A 100% • Vitamin C 16% • Calcium 4% • Iron 20% • **DIETARY EXCHANGES:** 1 Starch, 2 Vegetable, 3 Very Lean Meat **OR** 1½ Carbohydrate, 2 Vegetable, 3 Very Lean Meat

SERVE WITH

For casual entertaining, this one-pot meal is ideal. A basket of freshly baked breadsticks and a crisp green salad are all you need to round it out.

beef ragout on polenta

YIELD: 5 SERVINGS

Prep Time: 20 minutes (Ready in 10 hours 20 minutes)

½ cup chopped onion

1 green bell pepper, chopped

2 medium carrots, chopped

1 lb. beef stew meat

½ teaspoon coarsely ground black pepper

1 (14-oz.) jar tomato pasta sauce

1 (24-oz.) pkg. polenta, cut into 10 slices

1. In 4- to 6-quart slow cooker, layer onion, bell pepper, carrots, beef, pepper and pasta sauce.

2. Cover; cook on low setting for 8 to 10 hours.

3. About 10 minutes before serving, heat polenta as directed on package. Arrange 2 warm polenta slices on each individual serving plate. Top each with about 1 cup beef mixture.

NUTRITION INFORMATION PER SERVING: Serving Size: ⅕ of Recipe • Calories 290 • Calories from Fat 60 • % Daily Value: Total Fat 7g 11% • Saturated Fat 2g 10% • Cholesterol 60mg 20% • Sodium 750mg 31% • Total Carbohydrate 33g 11% • Dietary Fiber 4g 16% • Sugars 4g • Protein 24g • Vitamin A 180% • Vitamin C 40% • Calcium 4% • Iron 20% • **DIETARY EXCHANGES:** 2 Starch, 1 Vegetable, 2 Lean Meat **OR** 2 Carbohydrate, 1 Vegetable, 2 Lean Meat

SERVE WITH

For a change of pace from the polenta, serve this thick and chunky stewlike mixture over corn muffins, split in half, or wedges of corn bread.

burgundy beef and mushrooms

YIELD: 8 SERVINGS

Prep Time: 15 minutes (Ready in 7 hours 45 minutes)

4 slices bacon

2 lb. beef stew meat

2 large carrots, cut into 1-inch chunks

1 medium onion, sliced

½ cup all-purpose flour

½ teaspoon dried marjoram leaves

¼ teaspoon garlic powder

¼ teaspoon pepper

1 (10½-oz.) can condensed beef broth

½ cup dry red wine or nonalcoholic red wine

1 tablespoon Worcestershire sauce

1 (8-oz.) pkg. (3 cups) sliced fresh mushrooms

1 (16-oz.) pkg. uncooked egg noodles

2 tablespoons chopped fresh parsley

1. Cook bacon until crisp. Drain on paper towels; crumble. In 3½- to 4-quart slow cooker, combine bacon, beef, carrots and onion.

2. In small bowl, combine flour, marjoram, garlic powder and pepper. With wire whisk, stir in broth, wine and Worcestershire sauce until smooth. Add to beef mixture in slow cooker; stir to combine.

3. Cover; cook on high setting for 1 hour.

4. Reduce heat setting to low; cook an additional 5 to 6 hours.

5. About 30 minutes before serving, add mushrooms to beef mixture. Increase heat setting to high; cover and cook an additional 30 minutes or until mushrooms are tender.

6. Meanwhile, cook noodles to desired doneness as directed on package. Serve beef mixture over noodles. Sprinkle with parsley.

NUTRITION INFORMATION PER SERVING: Serving Size: ⅛ of Recipe • Calories 480 • Calories from Fat 110 • % Daily Value: Total Fat 12g 18% • Saturated Fat 4g 20% • Cholesterol 125mg 42% • Sodium 340mg 14% • Total Carbohydrate 53g 18% • Dietary Fiber 3g 12% • Sugars 5g • Protein 37g • Vitamin A 160% • Vitamin C 6% • Calcium 4% • Iron 35% • **DIETARY EXCHANGES:** 3 Starch, 3½ Lean Meat **OR** 3 Carbohydrate, 3½ Lean Meat

DOUGHBOY TIP

Did you know that you can reduce the slow-cooking time for this recipe by starting the cooker on high? Each hour of slow cooking on high shortens the total cooking time by about an hour.

sauerbraten

YIELD: 6 SERVINGS

Prep Time: 20 minutes (Ready in 9 hours 35 minutes)

2 lb. beef stew meat

1 cup chopped onions

1 cup beef broth

1 cup red wine vinegar or cider vinegar

2 bay leaves

6 oz. (3 cups) uncooked spaetzle or egg noodles

¾ cup crushed gingersnaps (about 15 cookies)

2 tablespoons brown sugar

2 tablespoons chopped fresh parsley

1. In 3½- to 4-quart slow cooker, combine beef, onions, broth, vinegar and bay leaves; mix well.

2. Cover; cook on low setting for 7 to 9 hours.

3. About 15 minutes before serving, cook spaetzle as directed on package. Remove bay leaves from beef mixture. Stir in gingersnaps and brown sugar. Cover; cook on low setting an additional 15 minutes or until mixture is bubbly and thickened. Serve beef mixture over spaetzle. Sprinkle with parsley.

NUTRITION INFORMATION PER SERVING: Serving Size: ⅙ of Recipe • Calories 430 • Calories from Fat 100 • % Daily Value: Total Fat 11g 17% • Saturated Fat 4g 20% • Cholesterol 130mg 43% • Sodium 320mg 13% • Total Carbohydrate 43g 14% • Dietary Fiber 2g 8% • Sugars 14g • Protein 39g • Vitamin A 0% • Vitamin C 4% • Calcium 4% • Iron 35% • **DIETARY EXCHANGES:** 2½ Starch, ½ Fruit, 4½ Very Lean Meat **OR** 3 Carbohydrate, 4½ Very Lean Meat

SERVE WITH

This traditional German dish is usually served with tiny dumplings called spaetzle, but hot cooked noodles or boiled potatoes would also be great accompaniments. Complete the meal with cooked cabbage, thick slices of dark rye bread and warm apple strudel for dessert.

rosemary beef and tomatoes

YIELD: 6 SERVINGS
Prep Time: 15 minutes (Ready in 10 hours 25 minutes)

2 tablespoons margarine or butter, melted

½ cup chopped onion

1 teaspoon beef base

½ teaspoon salt

¼ teaspoon pepper

1½ lb. beef stew meat

4 Italian plum tomatoes, chopped

1 tablespoon chopped fresh rosemary

6 servings prepared instant mashed potatoes

1. In 4- to 6-quart slow cooker, combine margarine, onion, beef base, salt, pepper and beef; mix well.

2. Cover; cook on low setting for 9 to 10 hours.

3. About 10 minutes before serving, stir tomatoes and rosemary into beef mixture. Increase heat setting to high; cover and cook an additional 10 minutes.

4. Meanwhile, prepare mashed potatoes as directed on package. Serve beef mixture over potatoes.

NUTRITION INFORMATION PER SERVING: Serving Size: ⅙ of Recipe • Calories 260 • Calories from Fat 155 • % Daily Value: Total Fat 17g 26% • Saturated Fat 6g 30% • Cholesterol 70mg 23% • Sodium 520mg 22% • Total Carbohydrate 4g 1% • Dietary Fiber 1g 4% • Sugars 2g • Protein 24g • Vitamin A 48% • Vitamin C 4% • Calcium 0% • Iron 15% • **DIETARY EXCHANGES:** 1 Vegetable, 3 Medium-Fat Meat

SERVE WITH
This full-of-flavor dish goes great with mashed potatoes, and it's also delicious over hot cooked noodles, fluffy white rice or steaming baked potatoes.

beef and bean tamale pie

YIELD: 4 SERVINGS
Prep Time: 15 minutes (Ready in 6 hours 15 minutes)

½ lb. lean ground beef

½ cup chopped onion

1 (15- or 15.5-oz.) can kidney beans, drained, rinsed

1 (10-oz.) can enchilada sauce

1 (6.5-oz.) pouch golden corn muffin and bread mix

⅓ cup milk

2 tablespoons margarine or butter, melted

1 egg

2 oz. (½ cup) shredded colby-Monterey Jack cheese

1 (4.5-oz.) can chopped green chiles

¼ cup sour cream

¼ cup chopped green onions

1. In large skillet, cook ground beef and onion over medium heat for 5 to 7 minutes or until beef is thoroughly cooked, stirring frequently. Drain. Stir in beans and enchilada sauce. Place beef mixture in 3½- to 4½-quart slow cooker.

2. In small bowl, combine corn muffin mix, milk, margarine and egg; stir just until moistened. (Batter will be lumpy.) Add cheese and chiles; stir gently to mix. Spoon over beef mixture in slow cooker.

3. Cover; cook on low setting for 5 to 6 hours or until toothpick inserted in center of corn bread comes out clean. Top individual servings with sour cream and onions.

NUTRITION INFORMATION PER SERVING: Serving Size: ¼ of Recipe • Calories 615 • Calories from Fat 260 • % Daily Value: Total Fat 29g 45% • Saturated Fat 11g 55% • Cholesterol 115mg 38% • Sodium 1340mg 56% • Total Carbohydrate 69g 23% • Dietary Fiber 10g 40% • Sugars 22g • Protein 30g • Vitamin A 30% • Vitamin C 22% • Calcium 26% • Iron 38% • **DIETARY EXCHANGES:** 4½ Starch, 2 High-Fat Meat, 1 Fat **OR** 4½ Carbohydrate, 2 High-Fat Meat, 1 Fat

DOUGHBOY TIP
Although the corn bread in this recipe won't brown like traditional baked corn bread, it will darken as the tamale mixture soaks into the corn-bread mixture. To be sure the corn bread is done, test with a toothpick toward the end of the cooking time.

chili beef and beans

YIELD: 10 SERVINGS

Prep Time: 20 minutes (Ready in 4 hours 20 minutes)

2 lb. lean ground beef

1 cup chopped onions

1 (28-oz.) can baked beans, undrained

1 (15.5-oz.) can butter beans, drained, rinsed

1 (15- or 15.5-oz.) can kidney beans, drained, rinsed

1 (12-oz.) bottle chili sauce

2 (4.5-oz.) cans chopped green chiles

2 tablespoons brown sugar

3 teaspoons chili powder

1. In large nonstick skillet, cook ground beef and onions over medium-high heat until ground beef is thoroughly cooked, stirring frequently. Drain.

2. In 3½- to 4-quart slow cooker, combine beef mixture and all remaining ingredients; mix well.

3. Cover; cook on low setting for 4 hours.

NUTRITION INFORMATION PER SERVING: Serving Size: ¹⁄₁₀ of Recipe • Calories 380 • Calories from Fat 120 • % Daily Value: Total Fat 13g 20% • Saturated Fat 5g 25% • Cholesterol 55mg 18% • Sodium 1050mg 44% • Total Carbohydrate 41g 14% • Dietary Fiber 9g 36% • Sugars 15g • Protein 25g • Vitamin A 20% • Vitamin C 15% • Calcium 10% • Iron 15% • **DIETARY EXCHANGES:** 1½ Starch, 1 Fruit, 3 Lean Meat, ½ Fat **OR** 2½ Carbohydrate, 3 Lean Meat, ½ Fat

SERVE WITH

Chili con Crescents open-face sandwiches will soon become a family-favorite dinner. Heat oven to 425°F. Separate an 8-oz. can refrigerated crescent dinner rolls into 2 large rectangles; place in ungreased 15 x 10 x 1-inch baking pan. Gently press dough to cover bottom of pan; seal perforations. Bake 10 minutes or until golden brown. Spread about 2 cups of the chili mixture over baked crust. Sprinkle with 1 cup crushed corn chips and ¼ cup grated Parmesan cheese. Bake 5 minutes.

picadillo with apples and almonds

YIELD: 12 SERVINGS

Prep Time: 20 minutes (Ready in 4 hours 20 minutes)

2 lb. lean ground beef

1 cup chopped onions

1 cup raisins

2 teaspoons chili powder

1 teaspoon salt

¾ teaspoon cinnamon

½ teaspoon cumin

½ teaspoon pepper

2 garlic cloves, minced

2 medium apples, peeled, chopped

2 (10-oz.) cans diced tomatoes with green chiles, undrained

½ cup slivered almonds, toasted

1. In 12-inch skillet, cook ground beef and onions over medium heat for 8 to 10 minutes or until beef is thoroughly cooked, stirring frequently. Drain.

2. In 3½- to 6-quart slow cooker, combine ground beef mixture and all remaining ingredients except almonds; mix well.

3. Cover; cook on low setting for 3 to 4 hours. Stir in almonds before serving.

NUTRITION INFORMATION PER SERVING: Serving Size: ¹⁄₁₂ of Recipe • Calories 245 • Calories from Fat 115 • % Daily Value: Total Fat 13g 20% • Saturated Fat 4g 20% • Cholesterol 45mg 15% • Sodium 320mg 13% • Total Carbohydrate 18g 6% • Dietary Fiber 2g 8% • Sugars 13g • Protein 16g • Vitamin A 4% • Vitamin C 8% • Calcium 4% • Iron 12% • **DIETARY EXCHANGES:** 1 Fruit, 2 Medium-Fat Meat, 1 Fat **OR** 1 Carbohydrate, 2 Medium-Fat Meat, 1 Fat

DOUGHBOY TIP

Picadillo, the Mexican version of hash, is great to have on standby when you need an easy no-prep meal. Place 2 cups Picadillo with Apples and Almonds in a tightly covered container. Cover and refrigerate up to 4 days or freeze up to 4 months. To thaw, place the container in the refrigerator for about 8 hours. Use it to fill taco shells, or flour or corn tortillas.

beefy tortilla casserole

YIELD: 6 SERVINGS

Prep Time: 20 minutes (Ready in 8 hours 20 minutes)

1½ lb. lean ground beef

1 (14.5-oz.) can diced tomatoes with green chiles, undrained

1 (10¾-oz.) can condensed cream of onion soup

1 (1.25-oz.) pkg. taco seasoning mix

¼ cup water

6 (5- or 6-inch) corn tortillas, cut into ½-inch strips

½ cup sour cream

4 oz. (1 cup) shredded Cheddar cheese

3 tablespoons sliced green onions

1. Cook ground beef in large skillet over medium heat until thoroughly cooked, stirring frequently. Drain.

2. In 3½- to 5-quart slow cooker, combine ground beef, tomatoes, soup, taco seasoning mix and water; mix well. Add tortilla strips; stir in gently.

3. Cover; cook on low setting for 7 to 8 hours.

4. About 5 minutes before serving, spread sour cream over casserole. Sprinkle with cheese. Cover; let stand about 5 minutes or until cheese is melted. Sprinkle with onions.

NUTRITION INFORMATION PER SERVING: Serving Size: ⅙ of Recipe • Calories 470 • Calories from Fat 260 • % Daily Value: Total Fat 29g 45% • Saturated Fat 14g 70% • Cholesterol 100mg 33% • Sodium 950mg 40% • Total Carbohydrate 26g 9% • Dietary Fiber 3g 12% • Sugars 9g • Protein 30g • Vitamin A 26% • Vitamin C 12% • Calcium 26% • Iron 18% • **DIETARY EXCHANGES:** 2 Starch, 3 High-Fat Meat **OR** 2 Carbohydrate, 3 High-Fat Meat

KIDS CAN HELP

An easy way to get the kids involved in the cooking process is to let them cut the corn tortillas into strips. If they're not old enough to use a knife, they can use a pair of clean scissors. Don't worry if the strips aren't exactly the same size—they'll be close enough.

cheesy italian tortellini

YIELD: 4 SERVINGS

Prep Time: 15 minutes (Ready in 8 hours 30 minutes)

½ lb. lean ground beef

½ lb. bulk Italian pork sausage

1 cup sliced fresh mushrooms

1 (15-oz.) container refrigerated marinara sauce

1 (14.5-oz.) can diced tomatoes with Italian seasonings, undrained

1 (9-oz.) pkg. refrigerated cheese-filled tortellini

4 oz. (1 cup) shredded mozzarella cheese or pizza cheese blend

1. In large skillet, break ground beef and sausage into large pieces. Cook over medium heat about 10 minutes or until browned, stirring occasionally.

2. Spray 4- to 5-quart slow cooker with nonstick cooking spray. Combine meat mixture, mushrooms, marinara sauce and tomatoes in sprayed slow cooker; mix well.

3. Cover; cook on low setting for 7 to 8 hours.

4. About 15 minutes before serving, add tortellini to slow cooker; stir gently to mix. Sprinkle with cheese. Cover; cook on low setting for an additional 15 minutes or until tortellini are tender.

NUTRITION INFORMATION PER SERVING: Serving Size: ¼ of Recipe • Calories 575 • Calories from Fat 295 • % Daily Value: Total Fat 33g 51% • Saturated Fat 13g 65% • Cholesterol 135mg 45% • Sodium 1330mg 55% • Total Carbohydrate 39g 13% • Dietary Fiber 3g 12% • Sugars 12g • Protein 34g • Vitamin A 30% • Vitamin C 28% • Calcium 32% • Iron 22% • **DIETARY EXCHANGES:** 2½ Starch, 4 Medium-Fat Meat, 1½ Fat **OR** 2½ Carbohydrate, 4 Medium-Fat Meat, 1½ Fat

DOUGHBOY TIP

If you don't have a can of the diced tomatoes with Italian seasoning, substitute a can of plain diced tomatoes and ½ teaspoon dried Italian seasoning.

veal paprika

YIELD: 6 SERVINGS

Prep Time: 20 minutes (Ready in 8 hours 35 minutes)

3 tablespoons all-purpose flour

¾ teaspoon salt

1½ lb. veal stew meat

2 tablespoons oil

½ cup chopped onion

1 (8-oz.) can tomato sauce

1 (5-oz.) can (⅓ cup) evaporated milk

2 tablespoons paprika

1 tablespoon Worcestershire sauce

12 oz. (6 cups) uncooked egg noodles

1. In resealable plastic bag, combine flour and salt; shake to mix. Add veal; shake until evenly coated. Heat oil in large skillet over medium heat until hot. Add veal; cook about 10 minutes or until browned, turning occasionally.

2. In 3½- to 6-quart slow cooker, combine veal and all remaining ingredients except noodles.

3. Cover; cook on low setting for 6 to 8 hours.

4. About 15 minutes before serving, cook noodles as directed on package. Stir veal mixture; serve over noodles.

NUTRITION INFORMATION PER SERVING: Serving Size: ⅙ of Recipe • Calories 390 • Calories from Fat 90 • % Daily Value: Total Fat 10g 15% • Saturated Fat 3g 15% • Cholesterol 130mg 43% • Sodium 670mg 28% • Total Carbohydrate 50g 17% • Dietary Fiber 3g 12% • Sugars 5g • Protein 28g • Vitamin A 38% • Vitamin C 6% • Calcium 12% • Iron 24% • **DIETARY EXCHANGES:** 3 Starch, 1 Vegetable, 2½ Lean Meat **OR** 3 Carbohydrate, 1 Vegetable, 2½ Lean Meat

DOUGHBOY TIP

The flavor of paprika can range from mild to pungent and hot, and the color can vary from orange-red to a very deep red. Most supermarkets carry only mild paprika, so you might want to check at an ethnic market for a more flavorful, hotter Hungarian paprika.

honey-dijon pork roast

YIELD: 8 SERVINGS

Prep Time: 20 minutes (Ready in 8 hours 20 minutes)

½ cup chopped onion

2 apples, peeled, sliced

1 tablespoon honey

1 tablespoon Dijon mustard

½ teaspoon coriander seed, crushed

¼ teaspoon salt

1 (2- to 2½-lb.) rolled boneless pork loin roast

2 tablespoons water

1 tablespoon cornstarch

1. In 4- to 6-quart slow cooker, combine onion and apples. In small bowl, combine honey, mustard, coriander and salt; mix well. Spread on all sides of pork roast. Place pork over onion and apples.

2. Cover; cook on low setting for 7 to 8 hours.

3. Remove pork from slow cooker; place on serving platter. Cover with foil.

4. In small saucepan, blend water and cornstarch until smooth. Add apple mixture and juices from slow cooker; mix well. Cook over medium heat until mixture boils, stirring occasionally. Cut pork into slices. Serve pork with sauce.

NUTRITION INFORMATION PER SERVING: Serving Size: ⅛ of Recipe • Calories 250 • Calories from Fat 90 • % Daily Value: Total Fat 10g 15% • Saturated Fat 4g 20% • Cholesterol 85mg 28% • Sodium 180mg 8% • Total Carbohydrate 9g 3% • Dietary Fiber 1g 4% • Sugars 6g • Protein 31g • Vitamin A 0% • Vitamin C 4% • Calcium 2% • Iron 8% • **DIETARY EXCHANGES:** ½ Starch, 4 Lean Meat **OR** ½ Carbohydrate, 4 Lean Meat

DOUGHBOY TIP

To get the most flavor from your coriander seed, place it in a small plastic bag and crush it slightly with a rolling pin or the flat side of a meat mallet.

porketta with two potatoes

YIELD: 6 SERVINGS

Prep Time: 15 minutes (Ready in 10 hours 15 minutes)

2 medium dark-orange sweet potatoes, peeled, cut into ½-inch cubes (about 2½ cups)

2 Yukon Gold potatoes, cut into ½-inch cubes (about 2½ cups)

2 teaspoons fennel seed, crushed

1 teaspoon dried oregano leaves

1 teaspoon paprika

½ teaspoon garlic powder

½ teaspoon salt

¼ teaspoon pepper

1 (2-lb.) boneless pork loin roast

1 cup chicken broth

1. Place potatoes in 3½- to 4-quart slow cooker. In small bowl, combine fennel seed, oregano, paprika, garlic powder, salt and pepper; mix well. Rub into pork roast. Place pork on potatoes. Pour broth over pork and potatoes.

2. Cover; cook on low setting for 8 to 10 hours.

3. Remove pork from slow cooker; place on serving platter. Cut pork into slices. Serve pork with potatoes.

NUTRITION INFORMATION PER SERVING: Serving Size: ⅙ of Recipe • Calories 360 • Calories from Fat 110 • % Daily Value: Total Fat 12g 18% • Saturated Fat 4g 20% • Cholesterol 90mg 30% • Sodium 380mg 16% • Total Carbohydrate 27g 9% • Dietary Fiber 3g 12% • Sugars 4g • Protein 36g • Vitamin A 230% • Vitamin C 25% • Calcium 4% • Iron 15% • **DIETARY EXCHANGES:** 1½ Starch, 4½ Lean Meat **OR** 1½ Carbohydrate, 4½ Lean Meat

DOUGHBOY TIP

Rubbing the pork roast with the seasoning mixture the night before and refrigerating it does double duty. It saves time in the morning before you head out the door, and it allows the seasonings to flavor the pork. Wait, though, to cut the potatoes until just before placing them in the slow cooker so they don't discolor.

cranberry-orange pork roast

YIELD: 6 SERVINGS

Prep Time: 15 minutes (Ready in 9 hours 15 minutes)

1 (2½-lb.) boneless pork shoulder roast, trimmed of fat

1 cup sweetened dried cranberries

½ cup chicken broth

1 teaspoon shredded orange peel

½ cup cranberry juice cocktail

2 tablespoons cornstarch

1. Place pork roast in 3½- to 4-quart slow cooker. In small bowl, combine cranberries, broth, orange peel and ¼ cup of the cranberry juice cocktail; mix well. Pour over pork.

2. Cover; cook on low setting for 7 to 9 hours.

3. Remove pork from slow cooker; place on serving platter. Cover with foil. Pour juices from slow cooker into medium saucepan; if necessary, skim off any fat.

4. In small bowl, blend remaining ¼ cup cranberry juice cocktail and cornstarch until smooth. Stir into juices in saucepan. Cook over medium heat until bubbly and thickened, stirring constantly. Cut pork into slices. Serve pork with sauce. If desired, garnish with additional shredded orange peel.

NUTRITION INFORMATION PER SERVING: Serving Size: ⅙ of Recipe • Calories 330 • Calories from Fat 140 • % Daily Value: Total Fat 15g 23% • Saturated Fat 5g 25% • Cholesterol 85mg 28% • Sodium 150mg 6% • Total Carbohydrate 25g 8% • Dietary Fiber 1g 4% • Sugars 18g • Protein 24g • Vitamin A 0% • Vitamin C 10% • Calcium 4% • Iron 10% • **DIETARY EXCHANGES:** ½ Starch, 1 Fruit, 3 Medium-Fat Meat **OR** 1½ Carbohydrate, 3 Medium-Fat Meat

SERVE WITH

This dish is both easy and elegant—perfect for a weeknight meal or weekend guests. Steamed green beans and mixed-rice pilaf go wonderfully with the flavors of cranberry and orange. Pass a basket of warm-from-the-oven refrigerated dinner rolls, and you'll win rave reviews.

autumn pork roast dinner

YIELD: 6 SERVINGS

Prep Time: 15 minutes (Ready in 8 hours 15 minutes)

1 (1¾- to 2-lb.) rolled boneless pork loin roast

¼ teaspoon salt

⅛ teaspoon pepper

3 large dark-orange sweet potatoes, peeled, thinly sliced

1 medium onion, sliced, separated into rings

¾ teaspoon dried thyme leaves

1 quart (4 cups) apple juice

1. Sprinkle pork roast with salt and pepper; place in 3½- to 4-quart slow cooker. Place sliced sweet potatoes around and on top of pork. Top with onion. Sprinkle with thyme. Pour apple juice over onion.

2. Cover; cook on low setting for at least 8 hours.

3. Remove pork from slow cooker; place on serving platter. With slotted spoon, remove sweet potatoes and onion from slow cooker. If desired, serve pork and vegetables with juices from slow cooker.

NUTRITION INFORMATION PER SERVING: Serving Size: ⅙ of Recipe • Calories 380 • Calories from Fat 100 • % Daily Value: Total Fat 11g 17% • Saturated Fat 4g 20% • Cholesterol 90mg 30% • Sodium 170mg 7% • Total Carbohydrate 37g 12% • Dietary Fiber 2g 8% • Sugars 21g • Protein 34g • Vitamin A 260% • Vitamin C 20% • Calcium 6% • Iron 15% • **DIETARY EXCHANGES:** 1½ Starch, 1 Fruit, 4 Lean Meat **OR** 2½ Carbohydrate, 4 Lean Meat

SERVE WITH

Bake some large refrigerated buttermilk biscuits to soak up the flavorful gravy this one-dish pork roast makes on its own. Add a tossed green salad, and dinner is served.

pork and pineapple

YIELD: 6 SERVINGS
Prep Time: 20 minutes (Ready in 8 hours 25 minutes)

1½ lb. boneless pork loin, cut into cubes

1 (8-oz.) can pineapple tidbits in unsweetened juice, undrained

1 medium red or green bell pepper, cut into squares

3 tablespoons brown sugar

½ teaspoon ginger

¼ cup vinegar

3 tablespoons soy sauce

⅔ cup uncooked regular long-grain white rice

1⅓ cups water

3 tablespoons water

2 tablespoons cornstarch

1. In 3½- to 4-quart slow cooker, combine pork, pineapple, bell pepper, brown sugar, ginger, vinegar and soy sauce; mix well.

2. Cover; cook on low setting for 6 to 8 hours.

3. About 25 minutes before serving, cook rice in 1⅓ cups water as directed on package.

4. About 5 minutes before serving, in small bowl, blend 3 tablespoons water and cornstarch until smooth. Stir into pork mixture. Increase heat setting to high; cover and cook an additional 5 minutes or until thickened. Serve pork mixture over rice.

NUTRITION INFORMATION PER SERVING: Serving Size: ⅙ of Recipe • Calories 330 • Calories from Fat 80 • % Daily Value: Total Fat 9g 14% • Saturated Fat 3g 15% • Cholesterol 70mg 23% • Sodium 500mg 21% • Total Carbohydrate 35g 12% • Dietary Fiber 1g 4% • Sugars 14g • Protein 28g • Vitamin A 24% • Vitamin C 34% • Calcium 2% • Iron 12% • **DIETARY EXCHANGES:** 1 Starch, 1 Fruit, 1 Vegetable, 3 Lean Meat **OR** 2 Carbohydrate, 1 Vegetable, 3 Lean Meat

SERVE WITH

Your family will also love this sweet and tangy dish served with hot cooked noodles instead of rice. If you're tired of the standard noodle choices, try cellophane or rice noodles for a change of pace.

easy pork chop suey

YIELD: 5 SERVINGS

Prep Time: 15 minutes (Ready in 7 hours 30 minutes)

1 lb. boneless pork shoulder, cut into ¾-inch cubes

1 small onion, cut into ¼-inch wedges

1 (5-oz.) can sliced bamboo shoots, drained

½ cup purchased teriyaki baste and glaze

1 teaspoon grated gingerroot

1 (1-lb.) pkg. frozen broccoli, carrots and water chestnuts, thawed, drained

2 cups uncooked instant white rice

2 cups water

1. In 4- to 6-quart slow cooker, combine pork, onion, bamboo shoots, teriyaki baste and glaze and gingerroot; mix well.

2. Cover; cook on low setting for 5 to 7 hours.

3. About 15 minutes before serving, stir vegetables into pork mixture. Increase heat setting to high; cover and cook an additional 10 to 15 minutes or until vegetables are tender.

4. Meanwhile, cook rice in 2 cups water as directed on package. Serve pork mixture over rice.

NUTRITION INFORMATION PER SERVING: Serving Size: ⅕ of Recipe • Calories 430 • Calories from Fat 130 • % Daily Value: Total Fat 14g 22% • Saturated Fat 5g 25% • Cholesterol 55mg 18% • Sodium 1180mg 49% • Total Carbohydrate 54g 18% • Dietary Fiber 3g 12% • Sugars 16g • Protein 21g • Vitamin A 45% • Vitamin C 20% • Calcium 10% • Iron 25% • **DIETARY EXCHANGES:** 2½ Starch, 1 Fruit, 1 Vegetable, 2 Lean Meat, 1 Fat **OR** 3½ Carbohydrate, 1 Vegetable, 2 Lean Meat, 1 Fat

DOUGHBOY TIP

Tightly covered, fresh gingerroot can be refrigerated for up to a week. For longer storage, freeze it in a covered container. To use frozen gingerroot, simply grate the amount you need and return the rest to the freezer.

pork chops with spiced fruit stuffing

YIELD: 4 SERVINGS
Prep Time: 10 minutes (Ready in 6 hours 10 minutes)

1 cup diced dried fruit and raisin mixture

1 cup chicken broth

½ cup apple juice

3 tablespoons margarine or butter

¼ teaspoon cinnamon

⅛ teaspoon nutmeg

1 (6-oz.) pkg. herb-seasoned one-step stuffing mix

4 (4-oz.) boneless pork loin chops (about ½ inch thick)

⅛ teaspoon salt

⅛ teaspoon pepper

1. In large saucepan, combine dried fruits, broth, ¼ cup of the apple juice, margarine, cinnamon and nutmeg. Bring to a boil. Stir in stuffing mix. Remove from heat.

2. Arrange pork chops in bottom of 3½- to 4-quart slow cooker. Pour remaining ¼ cup apple juice over pork. Sprinkle with salt and pepper. Top with stuffing mixture.

3. Cover; cook on low setting for 5 to 6 hours.

4. Remove stuffing from slow cooker; place in serving bowl. Stir gently; serve with pork stuffing.

NUTRITION INFORMATION PER SERVING: Serving Size: ¼ of Recipe • Calories 510 • Calories from Fat 160 • % Daily Value: Total Fat 18g 28% • Saturated Fat 4g 20% • Cholesterol 60mg 20% • Sodium 1000mg 42% • Total Carbohydrate 60g 20% • Dietary Fiber 6g 24% • Sugars 18g • Protein 28g • Vitamin A 25% • Vitamin C 2% • Calcium 6% • Iron 20% • **DIETARY EXCHANGES:** 3 Starch, 1 Fruit, 2½ Lean Meat, 1½ Fat **OR** 4 Carbohydrate, 2½ Lean Meat, 1½ Fat

DOUGHBOY TIP
If a package of the dried fruit mixture isn't handy, use 1 cup of your favorite chopped dried fruit, such as apples or apricots, instead.

pizza pork chops

YIELD: 6 SERVINGS

Prep Time: 15 minutes (Ready in 6 hours 15 minutes)

6 (6-oz.) pork loin chops (about 1 inch thick)

$1/2$ teaspoon salt

$1/4$ teaspoon pepper

1 tablespoon oil

$1/2$ cup chopped onion

2 cups tomato pasta sauce

4 oz. (1 cup) shredded mozzarella cheese

1. Sprinkle pork chops with salt and pepper. Heat oil in 12-inch skillet over medium-high heat until hot. Add pork; cook about 5 minutes or until browned, turning once.

2. Place pork in $3^{1}/2$- to 6-quart slow cooker. Sprinkle onion over pork. Pour pasta sauce over top.

3. Cover; cook on low setting for 4 to 6 hours.

4. Remove pork from slow cooker; place on serving platter. Top with sauce. Sprinkle with cheese.

NUTRITION INFORMATION PER SERVING: Serving Size: $1/6$ of Recipe • Calories 335 • Calories from Fat 135 • % Daily Value: Total Fat 15g 23% • Saturated Fat 5g 25% • Cholesterol 85mg 28% • Sodium 750mg 31% • Total Carbohydrate 18g 6% • Dietary Fiber 1g 4% • Sugars 7g • Protein 33g • Vitamin A 14% • Vitamin C 10% • Calcium 16% • Iron 8% • **DIETARY EXCHANGES:** 1 Starch, $4^{1}/2$ Lean Meat **OR** $4^{1}/2$ Carbohydrate, $4^{1}/2$ Lean Meat

SERVE WITH

Orzo, a tiny rice-shaped pasta, is a perfect partner to these pleasing pork chops. Pick up a packaged salad mix, and bake a batch of refrigerated garlic breadsticks to round out this casual Italian meal.

pork ribs with molasses-mustard sauce

YIELD: 6 SERVINGS

Prep Time: 15 minutes (Ready in 10 hours 15 minutes)

3¹⁄₂ lb. pork loin back ribs, pork spareribs or beef short ribs

¹⁄₂ teaspoon salt

¹⁄₄ teaspoon pepper

¹⁄₂ cup water

¹⁄₂ cup molasses

¹⁄₃ cup Dijon mustard

¹⁄₃ cup cider vinegar or white vinegar

1. Cut ribs into 2- or 3-rib serving portions; place in 5- to 6-quart slow cooker. Sprinkle with salt and pepper. Pour water over ribs.

2. Cover; cook on low setting for 8 to 9 hours.

3. About 1¼ hours before serving, remove ribs from slow cooker. Drain and discard liquid from cooker.

4. In large bowl, combine molasses, mustard and vinegar; mix well. Dip ribs in sauce to coat; place in slow cooker. Pour any remaining sauce over ribs. Cover; cook on low setting for an additional 1 hour.

NUTRITION INFORMATION PER SERVING: Serving Size: ⅙ of Recipe • Calories 585 • Calories from Fat 350 • % Daily Value: Total Fat 39g 60% • Saturated Fat 14g 70% • Cholesterol 150mg 50% • Sodium 660mg 28% • Total Carbohydrate 21g 7% • Dietary Fiber 0g 0% • Sugars 17g • Protein 38g • Vitamin A 0% • Vitamin C 0% • Calcium 12% • Iron 22% • **DIETARY EXCHANGES:** 1 Starch, ½ Fruit, 5 Medium-Fat Meat, 2 Fat **OR** 1½ Carbohydrate, 5 Medium-Fat Meat, 2 Fat

SERVE WITH

Strawberry Shortcakes are the perfect ending to an all-American rib dinner. Heat oven to 350°F. Separate a 16.3-oz. can large refrigerated home-style biscuits into 8 biscuits. Dip top and sides of each biscuit into 2 tablespoons melted margarine and then into granulated sugar. Bake 13 to 17 minutes or until golden brown. Cool slightly; split each biscuit. Divide 4 cups sliced strawberries among the biscuits, and top with whipped cream. Yum!

slow-and-easy barbecued ribs

YIELD: 6 SERVINGS

Prep Time: 10 minutes (Ready in 10 hours 40 minutes)

2 lb. boneless country-style pork loin ribs

1 medium onion, sliced

1 garlic clove, minced

⅔ cup barbecue sauce

⅓ cup plum jam

1. Spray 4- to 6-quart slow cooker with nonstick cooking spray. Place pork ribs, onion and garlic in sprayed slow cooker.

2. Cover; cook on low setting for 8 to 10 hours.

3. About 35 minutes before serving, drain and discard juices from slow cooker; wipe edge of cooker clean. In measuring cup, combine barbecue sauce and jam; mix well. Pour or spoon mixture over ribs, coating evenly.

4. Increase heat setting to high; cover and cook an additional 25 to 30 minutes or until ribs are glazed. Serve ribs with sauce.

NUTRITION INFORMATION PER SERVING: Serving Size: ⅙ of Recipe • Calories 440 • Calories from Fat 260 • % Daily Value: Total Fat 29g 45% • Saturated Fat 11g 55% • Cholesterol 105mg 35% • Sodium 290mg 12% • Total Carbohydrate 18g 6% • Dietary Fiber 1g 4% • Sugars 10g • Protein 27g • Vitamin A 6% • Vitamin C 6% • Calcium 4% • Iron 8% • **DIETARY EXCHANGES:** 1 Fruit, 4 Medium-Fat Meat, 1½ Fat **OR** 1 Carbohydrate, 4 Medium-Fat Meat, 1½ Fat

DOUGHBOY TIP

Make no bones about it: country-style ribs, cut from the loin, are the meatiest type of rib. Boneless country-style ribs are ideal for small slow cookers, and bone-in ribs can be used in large cookers.

key west ribs

YIELD: 4 SERVINGS

Prep Time: 10 minutes (Ready in 9 hours 10 minutes)

2½ lb. country-style pork loin ribs

¼ cup finely chopped onion

¼ cup barbecue sauce

1 teaspoon grated orange peel

1 teaspoon grated lime peel

½ teaspoon salt

¼ cup orange juice

2 tablespoons lime juice

1. Place pork ribs in 3½- to 4-quart slow cooker. In small bowl, combine all remaining ingredients; mix well. Pour over ribs.

2. Cover; cook on low setting for 7 to 9 hours. Spoon sauce over ribs.

NUTRITION INFORMATION PER SERVING: Serving Size: ¼ of Recipe • Calories 520 • Calories from Fat 350 • % Daily Value: Total Fat 39g 60% • Saturated Fat 14g 70% • Cholesterol 140mg 47% • Sodium 470mg 20% • Total Carbohydrate 5g 2% • Dietary Fiber 1g 4% • Sugars 2g • Protein 36g • Vitamin A 4% • Vitamin C 15% • Calcium 4% • Iron 10% • **DIETARY EXCHANGES:** ½ Fruit, 5 High-Fat Meat **OR** ½ Carbohydrate, 5 High-Fat Meat

SERVE WITH

Take a virtual cruise to the Caribbean by serving these citrus-flavored ribs with black beans and rice. Slices of fresh mango and pineapple make an easy and fresh dessert.

bolognese pasta sauce with spaghetti

YIELD: 6 SERVINGS

Prep Time: 15 minutes (Ready in 8 hours 45 minutes)

6 Italian sausage links (about 1½ lb.), cut into 1-inch pieces

1 cup finely chopped onions

3 tablespoons sugar

1 teaspoon dried basil leaves

1 teaspoon dried oregano leaves

½ teaspoon salt

2 garlic cloves, minced

1 (28-oz.) can crushed tomatoes, undrained

1 (15-oz.) can tomato sauce

1 (12-oz.) can tomato paste

12 oz. uncooked spaghetti

1. In 3½- to 4-quart slow cooker, combine all ingredients except spaghetti; mix well.

2. Cover; cook on low setting for 6 to 8 hours. Skim and discard fat, if desired.

3. About 30 minutes before serving, cook spaghetti to desired doneness as directed on package. Serve sauce over spaghetti.

NUTRITION INFORMATION PER SERVING: Serving Size: ⅙ of Recipe • Calories 560 • Calories from Fat 170 • % Daily Value: Total Fat 19g 29% • Saturated Fat 6g 30% • Cholesterol 55mg 18% • Sodium 1930mg 80% • Total Carbohydrate 78g 26% • Dietary Fiber 7g 28% • Sugars 17g • Protein 26g • Vitamin A 44% • Vitamin C 46% • Calcium 10% • Iron 32% • **DIETARY EXCHANGES:** 4 Starch, 3 Vegetable, 1 High-Fat Meat, 1 Fat **OR** 4 Carbohydrate, 3 Vegetable, 1 High-Fat Meat, 1 Fat

SERVE WITH

When you need an easy weeknight meal, this is it! While the spaghetti cooks, bake some refrigerated breadsticks and toss a Caesar salad. For dessert, serve spumoni ice cream and biscotti.

ravioli with smoked sausage and peppers

YIELD: 4 SERVINGS
Prep Time: 5 minutes (Ready in 6 hours 5 minutes)

½ (25-oz.) pkg. frozen cheese-filled ravioli

2 cups frozen bell pepper and onion stir-fry

1 (26-oz.) jar chunky tomato pasta sauce

½ lb. smoked sausage links, sliced

1 oz. (¼ cup) shredded fresh Parmesan cheese

1. In 3½- to 4-quart slow cooker, combine all ingredients except Parmesan cheese; mix well.

2. Cover; cook on low setting for 5 to 6 hours. Sprinkle individual servings with cheese.

NUTRITION INFORMATION PER SERVING: Serving Size: ¼ of Recipe • Calories 550 • Calories from Fat 270 • % Daily Value: Total Fat 30g 46% • Saturated Fat 13g 65% • Cholesterol 120mg 40% • Sodium 1380mg 58% • Total Carbohydrate 41g 14% • Dietary Fiber 3g 12% • Sugars 4g • Protein 30g • Vitamin A 10% • Vitamin C 10% • Calcium 30% • Iron 15% • **DIETARY EXCHANGES:** 2½ Starch, 1 Vegetable, 3 High-Fat Meat, 1 Fat **OR** 2½ Carbohydrate, 1 Vegetable, 3 High-Fat Meat, 1 Fat

SERVE WITH

For warm **Italian Biscuits,** separate a 12-oz. can refrigerated flaky biscuits into 10 biscuits. Mix together 3 tablespoons grated Parmesan cheese and 1 teaspoon dried Italian seasoning. Dip tops of biscuits into melted margarine and then into cheese mixture. Place cheese side up on ungreased cookie sheet. Bake as directed on can.

italian sausage lasagna

YIELD: 6 SERVINGS

Prep Time: 25 minutes (Ready in 8 hours 25 minutes)

¾ lb. bulk Italian pork sausage

½ cup chopped onion

2 (15-oz.) cans Italian-style tomato sauce

2 teaspoons dried basil leaves

½ teaspoon salt

1 (15-oz.) container part-skim ricotta cheese

1 cup grated Parmesan cheese

12 oz. (3 cups) shredded mozzarella cheese

12 oz. (12 noodles) uncooked lasagna noodles

1. In large skillet, cook sausage and onion over medium heat for 6 to 8 minutes or until sausage is no longer pink, stirring occasionally. Drain. Add tomato sauce, basil and salt; mix well.

2. In medium bowl, combine ricotta cheese, Parmesan cheese and 2 cups of the mozzarella cheese.

3. Spoon ¼ of the sausage mixture into 3½- to 5-quart slow cooker. Top with 4 noodles, broken into pieces to fit. Top with half of the cheese mixture and ¼ of the sausage mixture. Top with 4 noodles, remaining cheese mixture and ¼ of the sausage mixture. Top with remaining 4 noodles and remaining sausage mixture.

4. Cover; cook on low setting for 6 to 8 hours.

5. About 10 minutes before serving, sprinkle top of lasagna with remaining 1 cup mozzarella cheese. Cover; let stand about 10 minutes or until cheese is melted. Cut lasagna into pieces.

NUTRITION INFORMATION PER SERVING: Serving Size: ⅙ of Recipe • Calories 770 • Calories from Fat 335 • % Daily Value: Total Fat 37g 57% • Saturated Fat 18g 90% • Cholesterol 100mg 33% • Sodium 1980mg 83% • Total Carbohydrate 66g 22% • Dietary Fiber 4g 16% • Sugars 15g • Protein 47g • Vitamin A 36% • Vitamin C 18% • Calcium 90% • Iron 22% • **DIETARY EXCHANGES:** 3 Starch, 1 Low-Fat Milk, 2 Vegetable, 4 High-Fat Meat **OR** 4½ Carbohydrate, 2 Vegetable, 4 High-Fat Meat

DOUGHBOY TIP

Love your lasagna thick and meaty? For thick pieces of lasagna, use a 3½-quart slow cooker. A larger slow cooker will also work, but your lasagna pieces will be a bit thinner.

scalloped potatoes, tomatoes and ham

YIELD: 4 SERVINGS

Prep Time: 15 minutes (Ready in 7 hours 15 minutes)

6 cups thinly sliced, peeled potatoes (about 6 medium)

1/2 cup chopped onion

2 tablespoons all-purpose flour

1 teaspoon salt

1/4 teaspoon pepper

2 cups chopped cooked ham

1 (14.5-oz.) can whole tomatoes, undrained, cut-up

2 tablespoons margarine or butter, cut into small pieces

1. Spray inside of 3½- to 4-quart slow cooker with nonstick cooking spray. Layer half of potatoes, onion, flour, salt, pepper, ham, tomatoes and margarine in sprayed slow cooker. Repeat layers.

2. Cover; cook on high setting for 1 hour.

3. Reduce heat setting to low; cook an additional 5 to 6 hours. Stir before serving.

NUTRITION INFORMATION PER SERVING: Serving Size: ¼ of Recipe • Calories 390 • Calories from Fat 110 • % Daily Value: Total Fat 12g 18% • Saturated Fat 3g 15% • Cholesterol 40mg 13% • Sodium 1840mg 77% • Total Carbohydrate 56g 19% • Dietary Fiber 6g 24% • Sugars 6g • Protein 21g • Vitamin A 12% • Vitamin C 26% • Calcium 6% • Iron 12% • **DIETARY EXCHANGES:** 3 Starch, 2 Vegetable, 1 High-Fat Meat **OR** 4 Carbohydrate, 2 Vegetable, 1 High-Fat Meat

SERVE WITH

Just add a crisp green salad and **Chive Crescents** to complete this family-favorite dish. Separate an 8-oz. can refrigerated crescent dinner rolls into 8 triangles. Brush triangles with 1 tablespoon melted margarine. Sprinkle with ¼ cup chopped fresh chives. Roll and bake as directed on can.

ham and chicken enchilada casserole

YIELD: 8 SERVINGS
Prep Time: 15 minutes (Ready in 6 hours 15 minutes)

9 (5- or 6-inch) corn tortillas

1 (9-oz.) pkg. frozen Southwestern-flavored cooked chicken breast strips, thawed, chopped

1 cup chopped cooked ham

3 (4.5-oz.) cans chopped green chiles

1 (15.5-oz.) can great northern beans, drained, rinsed

8 oz. (2 cups) shredded Mexican cheese blend

½ cup chicken broth

1 (15- or 15.5-oz.) can kidney beans, drained, rinsed

1. Spray 3½- to 4-quart slow cooker with nonstick cooking spray. Layer 3 tortillas in bottom, overlapping. Top with half of the chicken, half of the ham, 1 can of the chiles, the great northern beans and ½ cup of the cheese.

2. Pour ¼ cup of the broth over layers. Repeat with 3 more tortillas, remaining chicken and ham, 1 can of the chiles, the kidney beans and ½ cup of the cheese. Top with last 3 tortillas, remaining 1 cup cheese, can of chiles and ¼ cup broth.

3. Cover; cook on low setting for 6 hours.

NUTRITION INFORMATION PER SERVING: Serving Size: ⅛ of Recipe • Calories 380 • Calories from Fat 115 • % Daily Value: Total Fat 13g 20% • Saturated Fat 6g 30% • Cholesterol 65mg 22% • Sodium 880mg 37% • Total Carbohydrate 43g 14% • Dietary Fiber 9g 36% • Sugars 4g • Protein 32g • Vitamin A 8% • Vitamin C 14% • Calcium 32% • Iron 30% • **DIETARY EXCHANGES:** 3 Starch, 3 Lean Meat **OR** 3 Carbohydrate, 3 Lean Meat

MAKE IT SPECIAL
Top off this casserole in the full Mexican style. Offer sour cream, chopped tomatoes, guacamole, salsa, shredded lettuce, sliced ripe olives and sliced green onions.

winter root and sausage casserole

YIELD: 6 SERVINGS

Prep Time: 20 minutes (Ready in 9 hours 20 minutes)

1 large baking potato, cut into $\frac{1}{2}$-inch cubes

1 large dark-orange sweet potato, peeled, cut into $\frac{1}{2}$-inch cubes

2 medium carrots, sliced

1 medium parsnip, sliced

$\frac{1}{2}$ cup chopped onion

1 lb. smoked sausage links, sliced

1 (14.5-oz.) can chunky tomatoes with garlic and Italian herbs, undrained

1 (14-oz.) can chicken broth

2 teaspoons sugar

$\frac{1}{2}$ teaspoon dried thyme leaves

$\frac{1}{4}$ teaspoon pepper

$\frac{1}{4}$ cup chopped fresh parsley

1. In $3\frac{1}{2}$- to 4-quart slow cooker, combine all ingredients except parsley; mix well.

2. Cover; cook on low setting for 7 to 9 hours. Stir in parsley before serving.

NUTRITION INFORMATION PER SERVING: Serving Size: $\frac{1}{6}$ of Recipe • Calories 430 • Calories from Fat 230 • % Daily Value: Total Fat 25g 38% • Saturated Fat 9g 45% • Cholesterol 50mg 17% • Sodium 1520mg 63% • Total Carbohydrate 29g 10% • Dietary Fiber 4g 16% • Sugars 8g • Protein 21g • Vitamin A 250% • Vitamin C 35% • Calcium 8% • Iron 15% • **DIETARY EXCHANGES:** 2 Starch, 2 High-Fat Meat, $1\frac{1}{2}$ Fat **OR** 2 Carbohydrate, 2 High-Fat Meat, $1\frac{1}{2}$ Fat

SERVE WITH

For a chill-chasing menu, serve this hearty casserole with warm biscuits and honey, plus mugs of hot orange-spiced tea.

moroccan lamb and rice

YIELD: 4 SERVINGS

Prep Time: 10 minutes (Ready in 9 hours 30 minutes)

1 lb. boneless lamb, cut into 1-inch pieces, or 1 lb. lamb stew meat

1 small apple, shredded

1 (6.9-oz.) pkg. rice and vermicelli mix with chicken seasonings

1½ cups chicken broth

1 teaspoon curry powder

¼ cup raisins

¼ cup slivered almonds

1. In 3½- to 4-quart slow cooker, combine lamb, apple, seasoning packet from rice mix, broth and curry powder; mix well.

2. Cover; cook on low setting for 7 to 9 hours.

3. About 25 minutes before serving, add rice and raisins; mix well. Increase heat setting to high; cover and cook an additional 20 minutes or until rice is tender. Sprinkle individual servings with almonds.

NUTRITION INFORMATION PER SERVING: Serving Size: ¼ of Recipe • Calories 430 • Calories from Fat 110 • % Daily Value: Total Fat 12g 18% • Saturated Fat 3g 15% • Cholesterol 75mg 25% • Sodium 1260mg 53% • Total Carbohydrate 50g 17% • Dietary Fiber 4g 16% • Sugars 11g • Protein 31g • Vitamin A 0% • Vitamin C 2% • Calcium 6% • Iron 25% • **DIETARY EXCHANGES:** 3 Starch, ½ Fruit, 3 Lean Meat **OR** 3½ Carbohydrate, 3 Lean Meat

SERVE WITH

For an authentic Moroccan touch, complement the meal with warm pita bread, hummus and a side of mango chutney.

lamb dijon

YIELD: 6 SERVINGS

Prep Time: 25 minutes (Ready in 10 hours 40 minutes)

¼ cup all-purpose flour

1 teaspoon salt

¼ teaspoon pepper

2 lb. lamb stew meat

2 tablespoons oil

6 small red potatoes (1¼ lb.), cubed

¼ cup Dijon mustard

½ teaspoon grated lemon peel

1 tablespoon lemon juice

2 teaspoons chopped fresh rosemary or ½ teaspoon dried rosemary leaves

2 garlic cloves, minced

1 (14-oz.) can beef broth

1½ cups frozen sweet peas, thawed

1. In resealable plastic bag, combine flour, salt and pepper; shake to mix. Add lamb; shake until evenly coated. Heat oil in 12-inch skillet over medium-high heat until hot. Add lamb; cook about 20 minutes or until browned, stirring occasionally. Drain.

2. In 3½- to 6-quart slow cooker, combine lamb and all remaining ingredients except peas; mix well.

3. Cover; cook on low setting for 8 to 10 hours.

4. Skim fat from juices in slow cooker. Stir peas into lamb mixture. Increase heat setting to high; cover and cook an additional 10 to 15 minutes or until peas are hot.

NUTRITION INFORMATION PER SERVING: Serving Size: ⅙ of Recipe • Calories 335 • Calories from Fat 110 • % Daily Value: Total Fat 12g 18% • Saturated Fat 3g 15% • Cholesterol 85mg 28% • Sodium 1060mg 44% • Total Carbohydrate 30g 10% • Dietary Fiber 4g 16% • Sugars 3g • Protein 31g • Vitamin A 4% • Vitamin C 12% • Calcium 4% • Iron 22% • **DIETARY EXCHANGES:** 2 Starch, 3½ Lean Meat **OR** 2 Carbohydrate, 3½ Lean Meat

SERVE WITH

Biscuit Flat Breads are easy to make. Heat oven to 400°F. Separate a 16.3-oz. can large refrigerated buttermilk biscuits into 10 biscuits. Place biscuits on ungreased cookie sheets. Press each into thin 6 x 5-inch oval; brush with beaten egg. Sprinkle with about ½ teaspoon sesame seed. Bake 6 to 9 minutes or until light golden brown and crisp. Cut into wedges, and serve warm.

beans 'n wieners

YIELD: 8 SERVINGS
Prep Time: 10 minutes (Ready in 6 hours 10 minutes)

1 lb. wieners, cut into fourths

3 (16-oz.) cans pork and beans in tomato sauce

½ cup ketchup

¼ cup finely chopped onion

¼ cup molasses

2 teaspoons prepared mustard

1. In 3½- to 4-quart slow cooker, combine all ingredients; mix well.

2. Cover; cook on low setting for 5 to 6 hours.

NUTRITION INFORMATION PER SERVING: Serving Size: ⅛ of Recipe • Calories 420 • Calories from Fat 170 • % Daily Value: Total Fat 19g 29% • Saturated Fat 7g 35% • Cholesterol 40mg 13% • Sodium 1540mg 64% • Total Carbohydrate 47g 16% • Dietary Fiber 10g 40% • Sugars 21g • Protein 16g • Vitamin A 10% • Vitamin C 6% • Calcium 10% • Iron 25% • **DIETARY EXCHANGES:** 2 Starch, 1 Fruit, 1½ High-Fat Meat, 1 Fat **OR** 3 Carbohydrate, 1½ High-Fat Meat, 1 Fat

KIDS CAN HELP

The kids will have fun shaping **Soft Pretzels.** Heat oven to 375°F. Unroll an 11-oz. can refrigerated breadsticks and separate into 12 breadsticks. Twist and stretch each breadstick to form 22-inch rope. Shape rope into pretzel shape; tuck ends under and press to seal. Place on ungreased cookie sheets. Brush pretzels with a beaten egg white. Sprinkle with grated Parmesan-Romano cheese blend. Bake 12 to 18 minutes or until golden brown.

busy-day chicken and turkey

Herbed Chicken and Stuffing Supper 56

Mango Chutney-Chicken Curry 57

Chicken in Wine Sauce 58

Chicken Fettuccine Alfredo 60

Chicken Italiano 61

Chicken Breasts Supreme 62

Spanish Chicken 63

Cajun-Seasoned Chicken 64

Thai Peanut Chicken 65

Chicken Stroganoff Pot Pie 66

Salsa Chicken 67

Chicken with Creamy Paprika Sauce 68

Five-Spice Chicken Big Bowls 69

Easy Chicken Cacciatore 71

Jambalaya with Red Beans and Rice 72

Chicken and Cornmeal Wedges 73

Smothered Buttermilk Chicken over Biscuits 74

Chicken Drumsticks with Sweet Potatoes and Pineapple 75

Sweet-and-Sour Chicken with Rice 76

Chicken Legs with Herbed Onion Sauce 77

Savory Turkey Breast 78

Turkey and Bacon Wild Rice Casserole 79

Turkey Breast with Bulgur and Feta Cheese 80

Turkey and Stuffing with Onion Glaze 81

Barbecued Turkey and Vegetables 82

Turkey-Rotini Casserole 83

Turkey and Bean Cassoulet 84

Turkey with Cornmeal-Thyme Dumplings 85

One-Pot Turkey Dinner 86

Ground Turkey and Beans 87

Southwestern Turkey 88

Turkey Drumsticks with Plum Sauce 89

SWEET-AND-SOUR CHICKEN WITH RICE, PAGE 76

herbed chicken and stuffing supper

YIELD: 6 SERVINGS

Prep Time: 15 minutes (Ready in 6 hours 35 minutes)

3 lb. bone-in chicken pieces, skin removed

1 (10¾-oz.) can condensed cream of chicken with herbs soup

4 medium dark-orange sweet potatoes, peeled, cut into ½-inch slices

1 (6-oz.) pkg. chicken-flavor stuffing mix

1¼ cups water

¼ cup margarine or butter, melted

1 cup frozen cut green beans, thawed

1. Place chicken pieces in 5- to 6-quart slow cooker. Spoon soup over chicken. Top with sweet potatoes. In medium bowl, combine stuffing mix, water and margarine; mix well. Spoon over sweet potatoes.

2. Cover; cook on low setting for 4 to 6 hours.

3. About 20 minutes before serving, sprinkle green beans over stuffing. Cover; cook on low setting an additional 15 to 20 minutes or until beans are tender.

NUTRITION INFORMATION PER SERVING: Serving Size: ⅙ of Recipe • Calories 620 • Calories from Fat 215 • % Daily Value: Total Fat 24g 37% • Saturated Fat 6g 30% • Cholesterol 150mg 50% • Sodium 1070mg 45% • Total Carbohydrate 52g 17% • Dietary Fiber 5g 20% • Sugars 16g • Protein 54g • Vitamin A 100% • Vitamin C 20% • Calcium 8% • Iron 22% • **DIETARY EXCHANGES:** 3 Starch, 1 Vegetable, 6 Lean Meat, 1 Fat **OR** 3½ Carbohydrate, 1 Vegetable, 6 Lean Meat, 1 Fat

DOUGHBOY TIP

Adding the green beans at the end of the cooking time keeps them green and crisp-tender. If you prefer, you can add the beans with the sweet potatoes, but they will be softer in texture and have a lighter green color.

mango chutney-chicken curry

YIELD: 4 SERVINGS

Prep Time: 20 minutes (Ready in 7 hours 20 minutes)

4 bone-in chicken breast halves (about 1¾ lb.), skin removed

1 (15-oz.) can garbanzo beans or chickpeas, drained, rinsed

1 small onion, thinly sliced

1 small red bell pepper, chopped (½ cup)

1 cup fresh sugar snap peas

1 (9-oz.) jar mango chutney

¾ cup water

2 tablespoons cornstarch

1½ teaspoons curry powder

¼ teaspoon salt

¼ teaspoon pepper

1. In 3½- to 4-quart slow cooker, layer chicken breast halves, beans, onion, bell pepper and sugar snap peas. In small bowl, combine all remaining ingredients; mix well. Pour into slow cooker.

2. Cover; cook on low setting for 6 to 7 hours.

NUTRITION INFORMATION PER SERVING: Serving Size: ¼ of Recipe • Calories 405 • Calories from Fat 65 • % Daily Value: Total Fat 7g 11% • Saturated Fat 1g 5% • Cholesterol 75mg 25% • Sodium 400mg 17% • Total Carbohydrate 58g 19% • Dietary Fiber 10g 40% • Sugars 23g • Protein 37g • Vitamin A 26% • Vitamin C 42% • Calcium 8% • Iron 26% • **DIETARY EXCHANGES:** 2 Starch, 2 Fruit, 4 Very Lean Meat **OR** 4 Carbohydrate, 4 Very Lean Meat

SERVE WITH

Serve this Indian-inspired meal over hot cooked rice or couscous. Offer small bowls of traditional curry toppers, such as toasted coconut, chopped peanuts, raisins and mango chutney, to pass at the table.

chicken in wine sauce

YIELD: 6 SERVINGS

Prep Time: 35 minutes (Ready in 9 hours 35 minutes)

4 slices bacon, cut into pieces	¾ cup red wine or nonalcoholic red wine
¼ cup all-purpose flour	½ cup chicken broth
½ teaspoon salt	2 teaspoons dried parsley flakes
⅛ teaspoon pepper	½ teaspoon dried thyme leaves
3 to 3½ lb. cut-up frying chicken, skin removed	½ teaspoon dried marjoram leaves
1½ cups fresh baby carrots	¼ cup water
1 cup frozen small whole onions, thawed	2 tablespoons all-purpose flour
1 (4.5-oz.) jar whole mushrooms, drained	2 tablespoons chopped fresh parsley
1 garlic clove, minced	

1. Cook bacon in large nonstick skillet over medium heat until crisp. Remove bacon from skillet; drain on paper towels. Refrigerate until needed.

2. Remove and discard all but 2 tablespoons bacon drippings from skillet. In shallow dish or pie pan, combine ¼ cup flour, salt and pepper; mix well. Coat chicken pieces generously with flour mixture. Add chicken to skillet; cook 7 to 10 minutes or until deep golden brown on all sides. Place chicken in 3½- to 4-quart slow cooker.

3. In same skillet, combine carrots, onions, mushrooms and garlic. Cook and stir over medium heat for 5 minutes or until lightly browned. Add to chicken in slow cooker. Add wine, broth, dried parsley, thyme and marjoram to same skillet; cook and stir until hot, scraping up bits from bottom of skillet. Pour over chicken and vegetables in slow cooker.

4. Cover; cook on low setting for 7 to 9 hours.

5. About 15 minutes before serving, with slotted spoon, remove chicken and vegetables from slow cooker; place on serving platter. Cover to keep warm.

6. In small bowl, blend water and 2 tablespoons flour until smooth. Stir into liquid in slow cooker. Increase heat setting to high; cover and cook an additional 8 to 10 minutes or until thickened. Sprinkle chicken with reserved bacon and chopped parsley. Serve chicken with wine sauce.

NUTRITION INFORMATION PER SERVING: Serving Size: ⅙ of Recipe • Calories 415 • Calories from Fat - 155 • % Daily Value: Total Fat 17g 26% • Saturated Fat 5g 25% • Cholesterol 150mg 50% • Sodium 630mg 26% • Total Carbohydrate 17g 6% • Dietary Fiber 2g 8% • Sugars 7g • Protein 51g • Vitamin A 100% • Vitamin C 6% • Calcium 4% • Iron 18% • **DIETARY EXCHANGES:** ½ Starch, 2 Vegetable, 6½ Very Lean Meat, 2 Fat **OR** 1 Carbohydrate, 2 Vegetable, 6½ Very Lean Meat, 2 Fat

DOUGHBOY TIP

Wondering about what wine goes well in this dish? Merlot is a good choice. The color is not as deep as that of many red wines, so sauce made with Merlot won't have the purplish color of other red wine sauces. Serve the rest of the bottle with the meal.

chicken fettuccine alfredo

YIELD: 5 SERVINGS

Prep Time: 25 minutes (Ready in 6 hours 25 minutes)

1¼ lb. boneless skinless chicken thighs, cut into ¾-inch pieces

1 (4.5-oz.) jar sliced mushrooms, drained

½ cup roasted red bell pepper strips (from a jar)

2 tablespoons dry sherry, if desired

1 (16-oz.) jar Alfredo sauce

3 cups frozen cut broccoli

10 oz. uncooked fettuccine

2 tablespoons shredded fresh Parmesan cheese

1. In 3- to 4-quart slow cooker, layer chicken thighs, mushrooms and roasted pepper strips. Drizzle with sherry. Spoon Alfredo sauce on top.

2. Cover; cook on low setting for 5 to 6 hours.

3. About 25 minutes before serving, rinse broccoli with warm water to thaw; drain well. Add broccoli to chicken mixture. Increase heat setting to high; cover and cook an additional 20 minutes. Meanwhile, cook fettuccine to desired doneness as directed on package. Drain.

4. Stir cooked fettuccine into chicken mixture. Sprinkle with Parmesan cheese.

NUTRITION INFORMATION PER SERVING: Serving Size: ⅕ of Recipe • Calories 745 • Calories from Fat 385 • % Daily Value: Total Fat 43g 66% • Saturated Fat 23g 115% • Cholesterol 215mg 72% • Sodium 660mg 28% • Total Carbohydrate 51g 17% • Dietary Fiber 6g 24% • Sugars 4g • Protein 44g • Vitamin A 72% • Vitamin C 50% • Calcium 38% • Iron 30% • **DIETARY EXCHANGES:** 3 Starch, 1 Vegetable, 5 Lean Meat, 4½ Fat **OR** 3 Carbohydrate, 1 Vegetable, 5 Lean Meat, 4½ Fat

SERVE WITH

Did you ever think you could make fettuccine Alfredo in the slow cooker? You can, and it's both easy and delicious! Try it yourself, with warm focaccia bread and a salad of sliced tomatoes and fresh basil for a little taste of Italy.

chicken italiano

Prep Time: 25 minutes (Ready in 10 hours 25 minutes)

8 boneless skinless chicken thighs (1½ to 1¾ lb.)

½ cup chopped onion

½ cup halved pitted ripe olives

2 tablespoons capers

1 teaspoon dried oregano leaves

½ teaspoon salt

½ teaspoon dried rosemary leaves, crushed

¼ teaspoon garlic powder

1 (14.5-oz.) can diced tomatoes, undrained

¼ cup water

1 tablespoon cornstarch

1. Place chicken thighs in 3½- to 4-quart slow cooker. Top with onion, olives and capers. Sprinkle with oregano, salt, rosemary and garlic powder. Pour tomatoes over chicken.

2. Cover; cook on low setting for 7 to 10 hours.

3. About 15 minutes before serving, with slotted spoon, remove chicken and vegetables from slow cooker; place on serving platter. Cover to keep warm.

4. In small bowl, blend water and cornstarch until smooth. Stir into liquid in slow cooker. Increase heat setting to high; cover and cook an additional 5 to 10 minutes or until thickened. Serve chicken with sauce.

NUTRITION INFORMATION PER SERVING: Serving Size: ¼ of Recipe • Calories 365 • Calories from Fat 160 • % Daily Value: Total Fat 18g 28% • Saturated Fat 5g 25% • Cholesterol 125mg 42% • Sodium 820mg 34% • Total Carbohydrate 10g 3% • Dietary Fiber 2g 8% • Sugars 4g • Protein 43g • Vitamin A 10% • Vitamin C 14% • Calcium 10% • Iron 26% • **DIETARY EXCHANGES:** 2 Vegetable, 6 Lean Meat

SERVE WITH

Mozzarella cheese is the hidden treat in **Cheese Bursts.** Separate a 12-oz. can refrigerated flaky biscuit dough into 10 biscuits. Partially separate each biscuit into 2 layers; insert ¾-inch cube of mozzarella cheese and about 1 teaspoon chopped green onions into each opening. Place on ungreased cookie sheet. Press edges to seal well. Cut a deep X on top of each biscuit. Brush with melted margarine. Bake as directed on can.

chicken breasts supreme

YIELD: 6 SERVINGS

Prep Time: 25 minutes (Ready in 4 hours 40 minutes)

2 slices bacon

6 boneless skinless chicken breast halves
(about 1½ lb.)

1 (4.5-oz.) jar sliced mushrooms, drained

1 (10¾-oz.) can condensed cream of chicken soup

2 tablespoons dry sherry, if desired

3 oz. sliced Swiss cheese

1 tablespoon chopped fresh chives

3 cups frozen broccoli florets

1. Cook bacon in large skillet over medium heat until crisp. Remove bacon from skillet; drain on paper towels. Refrigerate until needed. Reserve bacon drippings in skillet.

2. Add chicken breast halves to bacon drippings in skillet; cook over medium-high heat for 3 to 5 minutes or until lightly browned, turning once. Transfer chicken to 4- to 6-quart slow cooker. Top with mushrooms. In same skillet, stir together soup and sherry. Spoon over mushrooms.

3. Cover; cook on low setting for 3 to 4 hours.

4. Top mixture in slow cooker with cheese slices. Sprinkle with chives. Crumble bacon over cheese. Increase heat setting to high; cover and cook an additional 10 to 15 minutes or until cheese is melted.

5. Meanwhile, microwave broccoli in covered microwave-safe dish on HIGH for 6 to 8 minutes or until crisp-tender.

6. With slotted spoon, remove chicken, broccoli and mushrooms from slow cooker; arrange on serving platter. Serve with cooking juices from slow cooker.

NUTRITION INFORMATION PER SERVING: Serving Size: ⅙ of Recipe • Calories 285 • Calories from Fat 110 • % Daily Value: Total Fat 12g 18% • Saturated Fat 5g 25% • Cholesterol 90mg 30% • Sodium 610mg 25% • Total Carbohydrate 11g 4% • Dietary Fiber 3g 12% • Sugars 2g • Protein 36g • Vitamin A 38% • Vitamin C 30% • Calcium 20% • Iron 10% • **DIETARY EXCHANGES:** 2 Vegetable, 4½ Very Lean Meat

DOUGHBOY TIP

Most recipes don't use chicken breasts for long, slow cooking because they can become dry and stringy. In this recipe, however, the chicken stays moist and tender because it is smothered with a creamy sauce and simmered just 3 to 4 hours.

spanish chicken

YIELD: 6 SERVINGS

Prep Time: 15 minutes (Ready in 8 hours 15 minutes)

1¾ lb. boneless skinless chicken breast halves,
cut into 1-inch pieces

1 lb. Italian turkey sausage links, cut into
1-inch pieces

1 large red bell pepper, chopped (1½ cups)

1 cup chopped onions

2 garlic cloves, minced

1 teaspoon dried oregano leaves

½ to 1 teaspoon crushed red pepper flakes

1 (28-oz.) can diced tomatoes, undrained

1 (6-oz.) can tomato paste

1 cup uncooked regular long-grain white rice

2 cups water

1 (14-oz.) can artichoke heart quarters, drained

1 (4-oz.) can sliced ripe olives, drained

1. Spray 3½- to 4-quart slow cooker with nonstick cooking spray. Combine chicken, sausage, bell pepper, onions, garlic, oregano, red pepper flakes, tomatoes and tomato paste in sprayed slow cooker; mix well.

2. Cover; cook on low setting for 6 to 8 hours.

3. About 25 minutes before serving, cook rice in 2 cups water as directed on package.

4. Just before serving, stir artichoke hearts and olives into chicken mixture; cook until thoroughly heated. Serve chicken mixture with rice.

NUTRITION INFORMATION PER SERVING: Serving Size: ⅙ of Recipe • Calories 490 • Calories from Fat 145 • % Daily Value: Total Fat 16g 25% • Saturated Fat 4g 20% • Cholesterol 125mg 42% • Sodium 1320mg 55% • Total Carbohydrate 48g 16% • Dietary Fiber 8g 32% • Sugars 9g • Protein 47g • Vitamin A 56% • Vitamin C 76% • Calcium 14% • Iron 30% • **DIETARY EXCHANGES:** 3 Starch, 1 Vegetable, 5 Very Lean Meat, 1 Fat **OR** 3 Carbohydrate, 1 Vegetable, 5 Very Lean Meat, 1 Fat

MAKE IT SPECIAL

For the ultimate Spanish touch, try pitted kalamata olives instead of the ripe olives. Kalamata olives are both salty and fruity, which adds real flavor flair to this unforgettable dish.

cajun-seasoned chicken

YIELD: 4 SERVINGS

Prep Time: 15 minutes (Ready in 9 hours 15 minutes)

3 slices bacon, chopped

½ cup chopped green bell pepper

¼ cup chopped onion

¼ cup chopped celery

8 boneless skinless chicken thighs (1½ to 1¾ lb.)

2 teaspoons dried Cajun seasoning

1 (14.5-oz.) can diced tomatoes, undrained

1. Cook bacon in large nonstick skillet over medium-high heat until crisp. Add bell pepper, onion and celery; cook 2 to 3 minutes or until crisp-tender, stirring frequently. With slotted spoon, spoon bacon and vegetables into 3½- or 4-quart slow cooker.

2. Sprinkle chicken thighs with 1 teaspoon of the Cajun seasoning; place in same skillet. Cook chicken 4 to 5 minutes or until browned on both sides, turning once. Arrange chicken and any remaining drippings over vegetables in slow cooker. Pour tomatoes over chicken. Stir in remaining teaspoon Cajun seasoning.

3. Cover; cook on low setting for 8 to 9 hours.

NUTRITION INFORMATION PER SERVING: Serving Size: ¼ of Recipe • Calories 360 • Calories from Fat 160 • % Daily Value: Total Fat 18g 28% • Saturated Fat 6g 30% • Cholesterol 125mg 42% • Sodium 350mg 15% • Total Carbohydrate 7g 2% • Dietary Fiber 2g 8% • Sugars 3g • Protein 45g • Vitamin A 10% • Vitamin C 26% • Calcium 8% • Iron 24% • **DIETARY EXCHANGES:** 1 Vegetable, 6 Lean Meat

SERVE WITH

Brimming with fiery flavor, this seasoned chicken is wonderful over hot cooked rice. Round out the meal with sides of buttered corn and watermelon slices.

thai peanut chicken

YIELD: 4 SERVINGS

Prep Time: 15 minutes (Ready in 9 hours 15 minutes)

8 bone-in chicken thighs (about 2 lb.), skin removed

¾ cup hot chunky-style salsa

¼ cup peanut butter

2 tablespoons lime juice

1 tablespoon soy sauce

1 teaspoon grated gingerroot

¼ cup chopped peanuts

2 tablespoons chopped fresh cilantro

1. Place chicken thighs in 3½- to 6-quart slow cooker. In small bowl, combine all remaining ingredients except peanuts and cilantro; mix well. Pour over chicken.

2. Cover; cook on low setting for 8 to 9 hours.

3. With slotted spoon, remove chicken from slow cooker; place on serving platter. Skim fat from sauce. Spoon sauce over chicken. Sprinkle with peanuts and cilantro.

NUTRITION INFORMATION PER SERVING: Serving Size: ¼ of Recipe • Calories 380 • Calories from Fat 215 • % Daily Value: Total Fat 24g 37% • Saturated Fat 6g 30% • Cholesterol 85mg 28% • Sodium 630mg 26% • Total Carbohydrate 9g 3% • Dietary Fiber 3g 12% • Sugars 0g • Protein 36g • Vitamin A 10% • Vitamin C 6% • Calcium 6% • Iron 18% • **DIETARY EXCHANGES:** 2 Vegetable, 4 Medium-Fat Meat, 1 Fat OR ½ Carbohydrate, 2 Vegetable, 4 Medium-Fat Meat, 1 Fat

SERVE WITH
A platter of hot cooked rice and a simple side of sliced cucumbers tossed with vinaigrette are all you need to make this a truly Thai meal.

chicken stroganoff pot pie

YIELD: 4 SERVINGS

Prep Time: 20 minutes (Ready in 5 hours 30 minutes)

1 (0.87- to 1.2-oz.) pkg. chicken gravy mix

1 (10½-oz.) can condensed chicken broth

1 lb. boneless skinless chicken breast halves,
cut into 1-inch pieces

1 (16-oz.) pkg. frozen stew vegetables, thawed,
drained

1 (4.5-oz.) jar sliced mushrooms, drained

½ cup sour cream

1 tablespoon all-purpose flour

1½ cups all-purpose flour

¼ cup chopped green onions

2 teaspoons baking powder

½ teaspoon salt

¼ cup shortening

¾ cup milk

1 cup frozen sweet peas, thawed

1. In 3½- to 6-quart slow cooker, combine gravy mix and broth; stir until smooth. Add chicken, stew vegetables and mushrooms; mix well.

2. Cover; cook on low setting for 4 hours.

3. About 1 hour 10 minutes before serving, blend sour cream and 1 tablespoon flour until smooth. Stir into chicken mixture. Increase heat setting to high; cover and cook 20 minutes.

4. Combine ½ cup flour, onions, baking powder and salt. With pastry blender or fork, cut in shortening until mixture resembles fine crumbs. Stir in milk just until moistened. Stir in peas. Drop dough by rounded tablespoonfuls onto chicken mixture. Cover; cook on high setting for 45 to 50 minutes or until toothpick inserted in center of topping comes out clean.

NUTRITION INFORMATION PER SERVING: Serving Size: ¼ of Recipe • Calories 595 • Calories from Fat 225 • % Daily Value: Total Fat 25g 38% • Saturated Fat 9g 44% • Cholesterol 90mg 31% • Sodium 1650mg 69% • Total Carbohydrate 58g 19% • Dietary Fiber 7g 29% • Sugars 8g • Protein 41g • Vitamin A 72% • Vitamin C 34% • Calcium 30% • Iron 28% • **DIETARY EXCHANGES:** 3 Starch, 2 Vegetable, 4 Med Fat Meat **OR** 3 Carbohydrate, 2 Vegetable, 4 Med Fat Meat

SERVE WITH

Comfort food doesn't get any better than this. Serve this chicken classic with hot dinner rolls and a spinach salad tossed with strawberries.

salsa chicken

YIELD: 6 SERVINGS

Prep Time: 10 minutes (Ready in 9 hours 10 minutes)

1 tablespoon oil

12 boneless skinless chicken thighs (about 2½ lb.)

1 teaspoon salt

½ cup chunky-style salsa

1 (15-oz.) can black beans, drained, rinsed

1 (11-oz.) can vacuum-packed whole kernel corn, drained

2 tablespoons chopped fresh cilantro

1. Heat oil in 12-inch skillet over medium-high heat until hot. Sprinkle chicken thighs with salt; add to skillet. Cook about 4 minutes or until browned, turning once.

2. In 3½- to 5-quart slow cooker, combine salsa, beans and corn; mix well. Top with chicken.

3. Cover; cook on low setting for 7 to 9 hours. Sprinkle chicken and vegetables with cilantro before serving.

NUTRITION INFORMATION PER SERVING: Serving Size: ⅙ of Recipe • Calories 440 • Calories from Fat 155 • % Daily Value: Total Fat 17g 26% • Saturated Fat 5g 25% • Cholesterol 115mg 38% • Sodium 980mg 41% • Total Carbohydrate 30g 10% • Dietary Fiber 6g 24% • Sugars 4g • Protein 48g • Vitamin A 6% • Vitamin C 6% • Calcium 10% • Iron 32% • **DIETARY EXCHANGES:** 2 Starch, 6 Very Lean Meat, 1½ Fat **OR** 2 Carbohydrate, 6 Very Lean Meat, 1½ Fat

MAKE IT SPECIAL

To add an extra splash of color, you can also use whole kernel corn with bits of red and green pepper. If you want a bit more spiciness, try a medium or hot salsa.

chicken with creamy paprika sauce

YIELD: 5 SERVINGS

Prep Time: 10 minutes (Ready in 8 hours 20 minutes)

10 bone-in chicken thighs (about 2½ lb.), skin removed

1 medium onion, sliced

3 tablespoons chicken broth

2 tablespoons paprika

½ teaspoon salt

3 tablespoons cold water

3 tablespoons cornstarch

1 (8-oz.) container sour cream with chives

1. Place chicken thighs and onion in 3½- to 6-quart slow cooker. In small bowl, combine broth and paprika; mix well. Pour over chicken. Sprinkle with salt.

2. Cover; cook on low setting for 7 to 8 hours.

3. About 15 minutes before serving, with slotted spoon, remove chicken and onion from slow cooker; place on serving platter. Cover to keep warm.

4. In small bowl, blend water and cornstarch until smooth. Stir into liquid in slow cooker. Increase heat setting to high; cook an additional 8 to 10 minutes or until thickened. Stir in sour cream. Pour sauce over chicken.

NUTRITION INFORMATION PER SERVING: Serving Size: ⅕ of Recipe • Calories 355 • Calories from Fat 190 • % Daily Value: Total Fat 21g 32% • Saturated Fat 9g 45% • Cholesterol 120mg 40% • Sodium 380mg 16% • Total Carbohydrate 10g 3% • Dietary Fiber 1g 4% • Sugars 3g • Protein 33g • Vitamin A 42% • Vitamin C 2% • Calcium 8% • Iron 18% • DIETARY EXCHANGES: ½ Starch, 4½ Medium-Fat Meat OR ½ Carbohydrate, 4½ Medium-Fat Meat

DOUGHBOY TIP

If you can't find sour cream with chives, sometimes labeled as "potato topping," use an 8-oz. container of sour cream and add 1 tablespoon chopped fresh or dried chives.

five-spice chicken big bowls

YIELD: 4 SERVINGS
Prep Time: 40 minutes (Ready in 8 hours 40 minutes)

8 bone-in chicken thighs (about 2 lb.), skin removed

2 garlic cloves, minced

1 cup chopped onions

2 medium stalks celery, sliced

2 teaspoons grated gingerroot

1 teaspoon Chinese five-spice powder

½ teaspoon salt

½ teaspoon grated lemon peel

2 (14-oz.) cans chicken broth

2 cups uncooked regular long-grain white rice

4 cups water

1. Place chicken thighs in 3½- to 5-quart slow cooker. Top with garlic, onions, celery, gingerroot, five-spice powder, salt and lemon peel. Add broth.

2. Cover; cook on low setting for 6 to 8 hours.

3. About 30 minutes before serving, cook rice in water as directed on package. With slotted spoon, remove chicken from slow cooker; cool until able to handle. Cut meat from bones; return meat to slow cooker. Discard bones.

4. Divide rice evenly into 4 large shallow soup bowls, spreading rice up sides of bowls. Add chicken and broth.

NUTRITION INFORMATION PER SERVING: Serving Size: ¼ of Recipe • Calories 755 • Calories from Fat 180 • % Daily Value: Total Fat 20g 31% • Saturated Fat 6g 30% • Cholesterol 140mg 47% • Sodium 1340mg 56% • Total Carbohydrate 86g 29% • Dietary Fiber 2g 8% • Sugars 2g • Protein 60g • Vitamin A 4% • Vitamin C 4% • Calcium 12% • Iron 44% • **DIETARY EXCHANGES:** 6 Starch, 5 Lean Meat **OR** 6 Carbohydrate, 5 Lean Meat

MAKE IT SPECIAL
Serving this dish in shallow soup bowls makes savory Far East chicken far from ordinary. For an accent, sprinkle sliced green onions or chopped fresh cilantro over each serving.

easy chicken cacciatore

YIELD: 4 SERVINGS

Prep Time: 25 minutes (Ready in 8 hours 25 minutes)

4 bone-in chicken thighs, skin removed

4 chicken drumsticks, skin removed

1 (15-oz.) can Italian-style tomato sauce

1 (4.5-oz.) jar whole mushrooms, drained

1 teaspoon dried oregano leaves

1 small onion, sliced

1 small green bell pepper, cut into 1-inch pieces

2 garlic cloves, minced

¼ cup water

2 tablespoons all-purpose flour

1. In 3½- to 4-quart slow cooker, combine all ingredients except water and flour; stir gently to mix.

2. Cover; cook on low setting for 6 to 8 hours.

3. About 15 minutes before serving, with slotted spoon, remove chicken and vegetables from slow cooker; place in serving bowl. Cover to keep warm.

4. In small bowl, blend water and flour until smooth. Stir into liquid in slow cooker. Increase heat setting to high; cover and cook an additional 5 to 10 minutes or until thickened. Stir well; spoon mixture over chicken.

NUTRITION INFORMATION PER SERVING: Serving Size: ¼ of Recipe • Calories 340 • Calories from Fat 150 • % Daily Value: Total Fat 17g 26% • Saturated Fat 4g 20% • Cholesterol 105mg 35% • Sodium 690mg 29% • Total Carbohydrate 14g 5% • Dietary Fiber 3g 12% • Sugars 8g • Protein 32g • Vitamin A 10% • Vitamin C 15% • Calcium 10% • Iron 15% • **DIETARY EXCHANGES:** ½ Starch, 1 Vegetable, 4 Lean Meat, 1 Fat **OR** ½ Carbohydrate, 1 Vegetable, 4 Lean Meat, 1 Fat

SERVE WITH

This dish is bursting with real Italian flavor. Noodles are a natural accompaniment, as are any long pasta such as fettuccine, spaghetti or linguine. Cook your favorite variety, and divide the cooked pasta among single-serving bowls. Spoon the chicken and sauce over the pasta, and garnish each serving with sprigs of fresh oregano or rosemary.

jambalaya with
red beans and rice

YIELD: 8 SERVINGS
Prep Time: 30 minutes (Ready in 8 hours 30 minutes)

½ cup chopped onion

¾ lb. boneless skinless chicken thighs, quartered

1 garlic clove, minced

1 medium green bell pepper, chopped (1 cup)

2 bay leaves

1 (15.5-oz.) can red beans, drained, rinsed

1 (6-oz.) can tomato paste

1 (14.5-oz.) can diced tomatoes, undrained

½ teaspoon salt

1 (12-oz.) pkg. frozen shelled deveined cooked small shrimp, thawed

½ lb. cooked kielbasa or Polish sausage, halved lengthwise, cut into 1-inch slices

4 cups uncooked instant white rice

4 cups water

1. In 4- to 6-quart slow cooker, layer onion, chicken, garlic, bell pepper, bay leaves, beans, tomato paste, tomatoes and salt.

2. Cover; cook on low setting for 6 to 8 hours.

3. About 10 minutes before serving, gently stir shrimp and sausage into chicken mixture. Remove and discard bay leaves. Increase heat setting to high; cover and cook an additional 5 to 10 minutes or until shrimp and sausage are hot.

4. Meanwhile, cook rice in water as directed on package. Serve meat mixture over rice.

NUTRITION INFORMATION PER SERVING: Serving Size: ⅛ of Recipe • Calories 440 • Calories from Fat 110 • % Daily Value: Total Fat 12g 18% • Saturated Fat 4g 20% • Cholesterol 130mg 43% • Sodium 900mg 38% • Total Carbohydrate 56g 19% • Dietary Fiber 5g 20% • Sugars 4g • Protein 28g • Vitamin A 20% • Vitamin C 30% • Calcium 8% • Iron 30% • **DIETARY EXCHANGES:** 3½ Starch, 2½ Lean Meat, ½ Fat **OR** 3½ Carbohydrate, 2½ Lean Meat, ½ Fat

MAKE IT SPECIAL
Present this popular Creole dish in shallow soup or pasta bowls. Scoop the beans and rice into each bowl, then top with the meat mixture. Garnish with strips of green bell pepper and a splash of hot pepper sauce.

chicken and cornmeal wedges

YIELD: 5 SERVINGS

Prep Time: 25 minutes (Ready in 10 hours)

1 teaspoon oil

1 lb. boneless skinless chicken thighs, cut into 1-inch pieces

1½ cups sliced celery

1½ cups fresh baby carrots

1 cup sliced fresh mushrooms

1 (1.8-oz.) pkg. dry leek soup mix

4 cups water

1 (10.8-oz.) can (5 biscuits) large refrigerated flaky biscuits

1 tablespoon cornmeal

1½ cups frozen sweet peas

¼ teaspoon pepper

1. Heat oil in medium skillet over medium-high heat until hot. Add chicken; cook and stir until browned.

2. In 4- to 6-quart slow cooker, combine chicken, celery, carrots, mushrooms, soup mix and water; mix well.

3. Cover; cook on low setting for 7 to 9 hours.

4. About 35 minutes before serving, separate dough into 5 biscuits; cut each into 8 wedges. Sprinkle wedges with cornmeal. Stir coated biscuit pieces into hot chicken mixture. Increase heat setting to high; cover and cook an additional 25 to 30 minutes or until biscuits are no longer doughy in center.

5. About 5 minutes before serving, microwave peas in covered microwave-safe dish on HIGH for 3 to 4 minutes or until hot.

6. Just before serving, stir peas and pepper into chicken mixture.

NUTRITION INFORMATION PER SERVING: Serving Size: ⅕ of Recipe • Calories 440 • Calories from Fat 170 • % Daily Value: Total Fat 19g 29% • Saturated Fat 5g 25% • Cholesterol 60mg 20% • Sodium 1220mg 51% • Total Carbohydrate 43g 14% • Dietary Fiber 4g 16% • Sugars 8g • Protein 24g • Vitamin A 200% • Vitamin C 15% • Calcium 6% • Iron 20% • **DIETARY EXCHANGES:** 2½ Starch, 1 Vegetable, 2 Lean Meat, 2 Fat **OR** 2½ Carbohydrate, 1 Vegetable, 2 Lean Meat, 2 Fat

SERVE WITH

For a quick family supper, serve this tummy-filling entrée with creamy coleslaw, a fresh-fruit salad and brownie sundaes for dessert.

smothered buttermilk chicken over biscuits

YIELD: 5 SERVINGS

Prep Time: 25 minutes (Ready in 8 hours 45 minutes)

1 lb. boneless skinless chicken thighs,
cut into ¾-inch pieces

3 medium carrots, sliced

⅓ cup chopped onion

½ cup water

2 tablespoons margarine or butter, melted

¼ teaspoon salt

¼ teaspoon pepper

1 bay leaf

1 (1.2-oz.) pkg. roasted chicken gravy mix

⅓ cup buttermilk

2 teaspoons all-purpose flour

1 cup frozen sweet peas, thawed, drained

1 (10.2-oz.) can (5 biscuits) large refrigerated
buttermilk biscuits

1. In 4- to 6-quart slow cooker, combine chicken, carrots, onion, water, margarine, salt, pepper and bay leaf; mix well.

2. Cover; cook on low setting for 6 to 8 hours.

3. About 20 minutes before serving, stir gravy mix into chicken mixture. Remove and discard bay leaf. In measuring cup, blend buttermilk and flour until smooth. Stir flour mixture and peas into chicken mixture; mix well. Increase heat setting to high; cover and cook an additional 10 to 15 minutes or until peas are cooked.

4. Meanwhile, bake biscuits as directed on can. Serve chicken mixture over split biscuits.

NUTRITION INFORMATION PER SERVING: Serving Size: ⅕ of Recipe • Calories 440 • Calories from Fat 190 • % Daily Value: Total Fat 21g 32% • Saturated Fat 5g 25% • Cholesterol 60mg 20% • Sodium 1170mg 49% • Total Carbohydrate 39g 13% • Dietary Fiber 3g 12% • Sugars 10g • Protein 23g • Vitamin A 250% • Vitamin C 10% • Calcium 8% • Iron 15% • **DIETARY EXCHANGES:** 2 Starch, ½ Fruit, 2½ Lean Meat, 2½ Fat **OR** 2½ Carbohydrate, 2½ Lean Meat, 2½ Fat

KIDS CAN HELP

This delicious dish is sure to be a hit with kids as well as adults. Let the kids separate the dough into individual biscuits and place them on the cookie sheet so they're ready to pop into the oven.

chicken drumsticks with sweet potatoes and pineapple

YIELD: 4 SERVINGS

Prep Time: 15 minutes (Ready in 10 hours 15 minutes)

2 medium dark-orange sweet potatoes, peeled, sliced (about 3 cups)

1 (8-oz.) can pineapple tidbits in unsweetened juice, undrained

1/2 cup chicken broth

1/4 cup finely chopped onion

1 teaspoon grated gingerroot, if desired

1/4 cup barbecue sauce

2 tablespoons honey

1/2 teaspoon dry mustard

8 chicken drumsticks (about 1 1/2 lb.), skin removed

1. In 3 1/2- to 4-quart slow cooker, combine sweet potatoes, pineapple with liquid, broth, onion and gingerroot; mix well.

2. In small bowl, combine barbecue sauce, honey and dry mustard; mix well. Coat chicken drumsticks well with barbecue sauce mixture. Arrange chicken in single layer over potato mixture in slow cooker, overlapping slightly if necessary. Spoon any remaining barbecue sauce mixture over chicken.

3. Cover; cook on low setting for 7 to 10 hours.

NUTRITION INFORMATION PER SERVING: Serving Size: 1/4 of Recipe • Calories 300 • Calories from Fat 50 • % Daily Value: Total Fat 6g 9% • Saturated Fat 2g 10% • Cholesterol 80mg 27% • Sodium 300mg 13% • Total Carbohydrate 34g 11% • Dietary Fiber 3g 12% • Sugars 25g • Protein 28g • Vitamin A 250% • Vitamin C 25% • Calcium 4% • Iron 10% • **DIETARY EXCHANGES:** 1 Starch, 1 1/2 Fruit, 3 Lean Meat **OR** 2 1/2 Carbohydrate, 3 Lean Meat

DOUGHBOY TIP

Of the many varieties of sweet potatoes, two types are common in most supermarkets. Dark-skinned sweet potatoes with deep orange flesh are more moist and sweet than the pale-skinned variety with light yellow flesh. For this recipe, the dark-skinned sweet potatoes are ideal.

sweet-and-sour chicken with rice

YIELD: 8 SERVINGS
Prep Time: 25 minutes (Ready in 10 hours)

1 (20-oz.) can pineapple chunks in unsweetened juice

1 cup fresh baby carrots, cut in half

½ cup chopped onion

3 garlic cloves, minced

1 teaspoon finely chopped gingerroot

2 lb. boneless skinless chicken thighs, cut into 2-inch pieces

½ cup reduced-sodium soy sauce

½ cup firmly packed brown sugar

1⅓ cups uncooked regular long-grain white rice

2⅔ cups water

1 medium red bell pepper, cut into 1-inch pieces

1 medium green bell pepper, cut into 1-inch pieces

¼ cup water

¼ cup cornstarch

Chopped fresh parsley, if desired

1. Drain pineapple, reserving juice. Place pineapple chunks in small bowl; cover and refrigerate.

2. In 4½- to 6-quart slow cooker, combine carrots, onion, garlic and ginger-root; mix well. Top with chicken. In small bowl, combine soy sauce, brown sugar and reserved pineapple juice; mix well. Pour over chicken.

3. Cover; cook on low setting for 7 to 9 hours.

4. About 35 minutes before serving, cook rice in 2⅔ cups water as directed on package. Stir pineapple and bell peppers into chicken mixture. Increase heat setting to high; cover and cook 20 minutes.

5. In small bowl, blend ¼ cup water and cornstarch until smooth. Stir into chicken mixture. Cover; cook on high setting for an additional 10 minutes. Stir parsley into rice. Serve chicken mixture with rice.

NUTRITION INFORMATION PER SERVING: Serving Size: ⅛ of Recipe • Calories 305 • Calories from Fat 55 • % Daily Value: Total Fat 6g 9% • Saturated Fat 2g 10% • Cholesterol 45mg 15% • Sodium 590mg 25% • Total Carbohydrate 48g 16% • Dietary Fiber 2g 8% • Sugars 40g • Protein 17g • Vitamin A 92% • Vitamin C 54% • Calcium 6% • Iron 14% • **DIETARY EXCHANGES:** 1 Starch, 2 Fruit, 1 Vegetable, 2 Very Lean Meat **OR** 3 Carbohydrate, 1 Vegetable, 2 Very Lean Meat

SERVE WITH
If you're taking this Asian favorite to a potluck or gathering, try serving it with chow mein noodles instead of rice. The noodles add a nice crunch, and there's no worry about keeping them hot.

chicken legs with herbed onion sauce

YIELD: 5 SERVINGS

Prep Time: 15 minutes (Ready in 5 hours 15 minutes)

10 chicken drumsticks (about 2 lb.), skin removed

2 cups frozen pearl onions, thawed

¼ cup dry white wine or chicken broth

¼ cup evaporated milk

2 tablespoons chopped fresh parsley or 2 teaspoons dried parsley flakes

1 teaspoon dried tarragon leaves

¼ teaspoon salt

¼ teaspoon dried rosemary leaves, crushed

1 (10¾-oz.) can condensed cream of chicken soup

1. Place chicken drumsticks in 3½- to 6-quart slow cooker. In medium bowl, combine all remaining ingredients; mix well. Pour over chicken.

2. Cover; cook on low setting for 4 to 5 hours.

NUTRITION INFORMATION PER SERVING: Serving Size: ⅕ of Recipe • Calories 210 • Calories from Fat 70 • % Daily Value: Total Fat 8g 12% • Saturated Fat 3g 15% • Cholesterol 87mg 29% • Sodium 640mg 27% • Total Carbohydrate 11g 4% • Dietary Fiber 1g 4% • Sugars 4g • Protein 24g • Vitamin A 10% • Vitamin C 4% • Calcium 6% • Iron 14% • **DIETARY EXCHANGES:** 2 Vegetable, 3 Very Lean Meat, 1 Fat

DOUGHBOY TIP

Save the time of having to spoon that extra fat off the top of the sauce before you serve it by removing the fat from the chicken legs before cooking.

savory turkey breast

YIELD: 12 SERVINGS

Prep Time: 15 minutes (Ready in 9 hours 15 minutes)

1 (6- to 6½-lb.) bone-in turkey breast

½ cup chopped onion

½ cup chopped celery

1 bay leaf

1 teaspoon salt

½ teaspoon coarsely ground black pepper

1 teaspoon chicken-flavor instant bouillon

½ cup water

1. Remove gravy packet or extra parts from turkey breast. Place onion, celery and bay leaf in cavity of turkey. Place turkey in 5- to 6-quart slow cooker. Sprinkle with salt and pepper.

2. In small bowl, combine bouillon and water; stir until dissolved. Pour over turkey.

3. Cover; cook on low setting for 8 to 9 hours. Remove and discard bay leaf before serving.

NUTRITION INFORMATION PER SERVING: Serving Size: ¹⁄₁₂ of Recipe • Calories 305 • Calories from Fat 115 • % Daily Value: Total Fat 13g 20% • Saturated Fat 4g 20% • Cholesterol 125mg 42% • Sodium 410mg 17% • Total Carbohydrate 0g 0% • Dietary Fiber 0g 0% • Sugars 0g • Protein 47g • Vitamin A 0% • Vitamin C 0% • Calcium 2% • Iron 8% • **DIETARY EXCHANGES:** 7 Very Lean Meat, 1 Fat

SERVE WITH

Make an easy holiday meal by serving slices of this moist and flavorful turkey with gravy, baked acorn squash and a tossed green salad. Add warm whole wheat rolls and cranberry sauce for a festive finish.

turkey and bacon wild rice casserole

YIELD: 5 SERVINGS

Prep Time: 25 minutes (Ready in 6 hours 25 minutes)

4 slices bacon, cut into 1/2-inch pieces

1 lb. turkey breast tenderloins, cut into ½- to 1-inch pieces

1 cup coarsely chopped carrots

½ cup coarsely chopped onion

½ cup sliced celery

1 cup uncooked wild rice

1 (10¾-oz.) can condensed cream of chicken soup

2½ cups water

2 tablespoons soy sauce

¼ to ½ teaspoon dried marjoram leaves

⅛ teaspoon pepper

1. Cook bacon in large skillet over medium heat until almost crisp. Add turkey, carrots, onion and celery; cook 2 minutes or until turkey is browned, stirring frequently.

2. Spoon mixture into 3½- to 4-quart slow cooker. Add all remaining ingredients; mix well.

3. Cover; cook on low setting for 5 to 6 hours.

NUTRITION INFORMATION PER SERVING: Serving Size: ⅕ of Recipe • Calories 390 • Calories from Fat 140 • % Daily Value: Total Fat 15g 23% • Saturated Fat 5g 25% • Cholesterol 75mg 25% • Sodium 1080mg 45% • Total Carbohydrate 33g 11% • Dietary Fiber 3g 12% • Sugars 4g • Protein 30g • Vitamin A 140% • Vitamin C 4% • Calcium 4% • Iron 15% • **DIETARY EXCHANGES:** 2 Starch, 3½ Lean Meat, 1 Fat **OR** 2 Carbohydrate, 3½ Lean Meat, 1 Fat

SERVE WITH

Parmesan Rosemary Crescents add a nice flavor touch to this turkey casserole. Separate an 8-oz. can refrigerated crescent dinner rolls into 8 triangles. Mix together 1 tablespoon softened margarine, 2 tablespoons grated Parmesan cheese and 1 teaspoon dried rosemary leaves, crushed. Brush mixture over each triangle. Roll and bake as directed on can.

turkey breast with bulgur and feta cheese

YIELD: 4 SERVINGS

Prep Time: 20 minutes (Ready in 5 hours 20 minutes)

1 cup uncooked bulgur or cracked wheat

¼ cup sliced green onions

1½ teaspoons dried oregano leaves

¼ teaspoon pepper

1 garlic clove, minced

1 (14-oz.) can chicken broth

3 tablespoons lemon juice

1 (2- to 2 1/2-lb.) bone-in turkey breast half

½ teaspoon salt

¼ cup pitted kalamata or Greek olives

1 oz. (¼ cup) crumbled feta cheese

1. In 3½- to 6-quart slow cooker, combine bulgur, onions, 1 teaspoon of the oregano, pepper, garlic, broth and lemon juice; mix well. Sprinkle turkey breast half with salt and remaining ½ teaspoon oregano. Place turkey on top of bulgur mixture.

2. Cover; cook on low setting for 4 to 5 hours.

3. Remove turkey from slow cooker. Cut turkey into slices. Stir olives and cheese into bulgur mixture. Serve turkey with bulgur mixture.

NUTRITION INFORMATION PER SERVING: Serving Size: ¼ of Recipe • Calories 510 • Calories from Fat 170 • % Daily Value: Total Fat 19g 29% • Saturated Fat 6g 30% • Cholesterol 155mg 52% • Sodium 1070mg 45% • Total Carbohydrate 30g 10% • Dietary Fiber 7g 28% • Sugars 2g • Protein 62g • Vitamin A 4% • Vitamin C 4% • Calcium 10% • Iron 18% • **DIETARY EXCHANGES:** 2 Starch, 8 Very Lean Meat, 2 Fat **OR** 2 Carbohydrate, 8 Very Lean Meat, 2 Fat

DOUGHBOY TIP

The best way to thaw a turkey breast is in the refrigerator. Allow about 24 hours for the 2- to 2½-pound turkey breast half in this recipe. Or you can use the cold water thawing method by placing the tightly wrapped turkey breast half in cold water. Allow 30 minutes per pound to thaw, and change the water often so it stays cold.

turkey and stuffing with onion glaze

YIELD: 6 SERVINGS

Prep Time: 15 minutes (Ready in 6 hours 15 minutes)

1 tablespoon margarine or butter

½ cup chopped onion

1 tablespoon apple jelly

1 (6-oz.) pkg. turkey-flavor one-step stuffing mix

¾ cup water

1 (2- to 2½-lb.) boneless skinless turkey breast half

Salt and pepper

1. Melt margarine in medium skillet over medium heat. Add onion; cook 4 to 5 minutes or until tender and lightly browned, stirring occasionally. Stir jelly into onion mixture. Cook an additional 1 to 2 minutes or until golden brown, stirring occasionally.

2. Meanwhile, spray 4- to 6-quart slow cooker with nonstick cooking spray. Place stuffing mix in sprayed slow cooker. Drizzle with water; mix gently. If desired, sprinkle turkey breast half with salt and pepper. Place on stuffing mix. Spoon onion mixture over turkey; spread evenly.

3. Cover; cook on low setting for 5 to 6 hours.

4. Remove turkey from slow cooker. Cut turkey into slices. Serve stuffing topped with turkey slices.

NUTRITION INFORMATION PER SERVING: Serving Size: ⅙ of Recipe • Calories 285 • Calories from Fat 35 • % Daily Value: Total Fat 4g 6% • Saturated Fat 1g 5% • Cholesterol 100mg 33% • Sodium 540mg 23% • Total Carbohydrate 25g 8% • Dietary Fiber 1g 4% • Sugars 3g • Protein 38g • Vitamin A 2% • Vitamin C 0% • Calcium 4% • Iron 16% • **DIETARY EXCHANGES:** 1½ Starch, 5 Very Lean Meat **OR** 1½ Carbohydrate, 5 Very Lean Meat

SERVE WITH

Steamed broccoli, cranberry relish and **Garlic Cheese Biscuits** make this a turkey dinner you'll want to serve year-round. Separate a 16.3-oz. can large refrigerated flaky biscuits into 8 biscuits. Place biscuits about 2 inches apart on ungreased cookie sheet. Mix 1 tablespoon melted margarine and ¼ teaspoon garlic powder; brush over biscuits. Sprinkle ¼ cup shredded Cheddar cheese over biscuits. Bake as directed on can.

barbecued turkey
and vegetables

YIELD: 4 SERVINGS

Prep Time: 20 minutes (Ready in 10 hours 20 minutes)

1 cup barbecue sauce

½ cup hot water

2 bone-in turkey thighs (1½ lb.), skin removed

3 medium potatoes, unpeeled, each cut into 8 pieces

6 medium carrots, cut into 2 1/2 x ½-inch sticks

1. In medium bowl, combine barbecue sauce and water; mix well. In 3½- to 4-quart slow cooker, layer turkey, potatoes and carrots. Pour sauce mixture over top.

2. Cover; cook on low setting for 8 to 10 hours.

3. With slotted spoon, remove turkey and vegetables from slow cooker; place on serving platter. Remove turkey meat from bones and cut into pieces; discard bones. Spoon cooking juices from slow cooker over turkey and vegetables.

NUTRITION INFORMATION PER SERVING: Serving Size: ¼ of Recipe • Calories 350 • Calories from Fat 35 • % Daily Value: Total Fat 4g 6% • Saturated Fat 1g 5% • Cholesterol 105mg 35% • Sodium 740mg 31% • Total Carbohydrate 53g 18% • Dietary Fiber 5g 20% • Sugars 23g • Protein 30g • Vitamin A 100% • Vitamin C 8% • Calcium 18% • Iron 24% • **DIETARY EXCHANGES:** 3 Starch, 2 Vegetable, 2 Very Lean Meat **OR** 3 Carbohydrate, 2 Vegetable, 2 Very Lean Meat

DOUGHBOY TIP

When time is tight, prepare the vegetables the night before and cover them with water. Before leaving the house in the morning, simply drain and discard the water, then combine the veggies with the other ingredients.

turkey-rotini casserole

YIELD: 4 SERVINGS

Prep Time: 15 minutes (Ready in 8 hours 50 minutes)

1 cup fat-free chicken broth with ⅓ less sodium

½ cup water

1 small stalk celery

½ teaspoon dried thyme leaves

1 bay leaf

2 bone-in turkey thighs (about 1½ lb.), skin removed

1 (1.25-oz.) pkg. Alfredo sauce mix

1 (10¾-oz.) can condensed 98% fat-free cream of mushroom soup

1 (9-oz.) pkg. frozen cut broccoli in a pouch, thawed, drained

8 oz. (about 2½ cups) uncooked rotini (spiral pasta)

½ cup grated Parmesan cheese

1. In 3½- to 4-quart slow cooker, combine broth and water. Add celery, thyme and bay leaf. Top with turkey thighs.

2. Cover; cook on low setting for 6 to 8 hours.

3. About 35 minutes before serving, remove turkey, celery and bay leaf from slow cooker; discard celery and bay leaf. Increase heat setting to high. In small bowl, combine sauce mix and soup; mix well. Stir into liquid in slow cooker. Stir in broccoli. Cover; cook on high setting for about 30 minutes or until thickened.

4. Meanwhile, cook rotini to desired doneness as directed on package. While rotini is cooking, remove turkey meat from bones and cut into pieces; discard bones.

5. Return turkey to slow cooker. Stir in cooked rotini and cheese.

NUTRITION INFORMATION PER SERVING: Serving Size: ¼ of Recipe • Calories 580 • Calories from Fat 135 • % Daily Value: Total Fat 15g 23% • Saturated Fat 6g 30% • Cholesterol 165mg 55% • Sodium 1730mg 72% • Total Carbohydrate 59g 20% • Dietary Fiber 4g 16% • Sugars 5g • Protein 56g • Vitamin A 22% • Vitamin C 20% • Calcium 28% • Iron 36% • **DIETARY EXCHANGES:** 3 Starch, 2 Vegetable, 6 Very Lean Meat, 2 Fat **OR** 4 Carbohydrate, 2 Vegetable, 6 Very Lean Meat, 2 Fat

DOUGHBOY TIP

Other shapes of similarly sized pasta can also be used in this casserole. Wagon wheels, mafalda (mini-lasagna noodles) and penne will work well, too.

turkey and bean cassoulet

YIELD: 6 SERVINGS

Prep Time: 20 minutes (Ready in 18 hours 25 minutes)

1½ cups dried great northern beans

1 lb. turkey breast tenderloins, cut into 1-inch pieces

1 medium green bell pepper, chopped (1 cup)

1 cup sliced celery

½ cup chopped onion

2 garlic cloves, minced

2 bay leaves

¼ teaspoon pepper

1 (14-oz.) can chicken broth

1½ cups water

1 (14.5-oz.) can diced tomatoes, undrained

¾ teaspoon salt

1. Place beans in medium bowl; add enough water to cover. Let stand at least 8 hours or overnight to soak.

2. Drain beans; discard water. In 3½- to 4-quart slow cooker, combine beans and all remaining ingredients except tomatoes and salt; mix well.

3. Cover; cook on low setting for 8 to 10 hours.

4. About 10 minutes before serving, stir tomatoes and salt into turkey mixture. Remove and discard bay leaves. Cover; cook on low setting an additional 10 minutes or until thoroughly heated.

NUTRITION INFORMATION PER SERVING: Serving Size: ⅙ of Recipe • Calories 280 • Calories from Fat 20 • % Daily Value: Total Fat 2g 3% • Saturated Fat 0g 0% • Cholesterol 50mg 17% • Sodium 640mg 27% • Total Carbohydrate 35g 12% • Dietary Fiber 11g 44% • Sugars 4g • Protein 31g • Vitamin A 10% • Vitamin C 30% • Calcium 10% • Iron 25% • **DIETARY EXCHANGES:** 2 Starch, 1 Vegetable, 3 Very Lean Meat **OR** 2 Carbohydrate, 1 Vegetable, 3 Very Lean Meat

MAKE IT SPECIAL

Serve cassoulet in **Biscuit Cups.** Heat oven to 375°F. Spray *outside* bottom and sides of eight 6-oz. custard cups lightly with nonstick cooking spray. Separate a 16.3-oz. can large refrigerated buttermilk biscuits into 8 biscuits. Press each biscuit to form 4½-inch round. Place rounds over outside of sprayed cups; press over bottom and part way down sides of cups. Place cups, dough side up, in 15 x 10 x 1-inch baking pan. Bake 14 to 16 minutes or until deep golden brown. Carefully remove biscuit cups from custard cups; fill with cassoulet.

turkey with cornmeal-thyme dumplings

YIELD: 4 SERVINGS

Prep Time: 15 minutes (Ready in 11 hours)

TURKEY

2 turkey thighs (about 1½ lb.),
skin and bones removed

1 (15.25-oz.) can whole kernel corn, undrained

1 (8-oz.) can tomato sauce

2 tablespoons all-purpose flour

1¼ teaspoons salt

1 teaspoon chili powder

¼ teaspoon pepper

1 medium zucchini, sliced (2 cups)

DUMPLINGS

¼ cup finely chopped onion

½ cup all-purpose flour

½ cup yellow cornmeal

1 teaspoon baking powder

¼ teaspoon salt

¼ teaspoon ground thyme

¼ cup milk

2 tablespoons oil

1 egg

1. Place turkey in 3½- to 6-quart slow cooker. In small bowl, combine corn, tomato sauce, 2 tablespoons flour, 1 teaspoon of the salt, chili powder and pepper; mix well. Pour over turkey.

2. Cover; cook on low setting for 8 to 10 hours.

3. About 50 minutes before serving, in medium bowl, combine all dumpling ingredients; mix well. Drop dough by spoonfuls onto hot turkey mixture. Arrange zucchini slices around dumplings; sprinkle with remaining ¼ teaspoon salt. Increase heat setting to high; cover and cook an additional 35 to 45 minutes or until toothpick inserted in center of dumplings comes out clean.

NUTRITION INFORMATION PER SERVING: Serving Size: ¼ of Recipe • Calories 510 • Calories from Fat 135 • % Daily Value: Total Fat 15g 23% • Saturated Fat 3g 15% • Cholesterol 190mg 63% • Sodium 1720mg 72% • Total Carbohydrate 56g 19% • Dietary Fiber 6g 24% • Sugars 9g • Protein 44g • Vitamin A 24% • Vitamin C 18% • Calcium 14% • Iron 36% • DIETARY EXCHANGES: 3 Starch, 2 Vegetable, 4½ Very Lean Meat, 1 Fat OR 3 Carbohydrate, 2 Vegetable, 4½ Very Lean Meat, 1 Fat

DOUGHBOY TIP
Be sure the turkey thighs are tender before you mix up the dumpling dough. If the dough stands too long before being added to the top of the turkey mixture, the baking powder will start to work and the dumplings may not be as light and fluffy.

one-pot turkey dinner

YIELD: 6 SERVINGS

Prep Time: 15 minutes (Ready in 8 hours 15 minutes)

3 medium dark-orange sweet potatoes, peeled, cut into 2-inch pieces

3 bone-in turkey thighs (about 2¼ lb.), skin removed

1 (12-oz.) jar turkey gravy

2 tablespoons all-purpose flour

1 teaspoon dried parsley flakes

½ teaspoon dried rosemary leaves, crushed

⅛ teaspoon pepper

1 (10-oz.) pkg. frozen cut green beans

1. Place sweet potatoes in 4- to 5-quart slow cooker. Top with turkey thighs. In small bowl, combine all remaining ingredients except beans; mix until smooth. Pour over turkey.

2. Cover; cook on high setting for 1 hour. Reduce heat setting to low; cook 5 hours.

3. One to 2 hours before serving, stir beans into turkey mixture. Cover; cook on low setting for an additional 1 to 2 hours.

4. With slotted spoon, remove turkey and vegetables from slow cooker; place on serving platter. Remove turkey meat from bones and cut into pieces; discard bones. Stir sauce. Serve turkey and vegetables with sauce.

NUTRITION INFORMATION PER SERVING: Serving Size: ⅙ of Recipe • Calories 340 • Calories from Fat 80 • % Daily Value: Total Fat 9g 14% • Saturated Fat 3g 15% • Cholesterol 155mg 52% • Sodium 460mg 19% • Total Carbohydrate 26g 9% • Dietary Fiber 4g 16% • Sugars 13g • Protein 43g • Vitamin A 100% • Vitamin C 16% • Calcium 8% • Iron 24% • **DIETARY EXCHANGES:** 1½ Starch, 1 Vegetable, 5 Very Lean Meat, ½ Fat **OR** 2 Carbohydrate, 1 Vegetable, 5 Very Lean Meat, ½ Fat

SERVE WITH

Just add **Onion 'n' Cream Crescents** to this one-pot meal. Heat oven to 375°F. Mix 3-oz. package cream cheese, softened, and 2 tablespoons chopped green onions. Separate an 8-oz. can refrigerated crescent dinner rolls into 8 triangles. Spread each with about 2 teaspoons cheese mixture. Roll as directed on can; place on ungreased cookie sheet. Brush with a beaten egg. Bake 12 to 15 minutes or until deep golden brown.

ground turkey and beans

YIELD: 12 SERVINGS

Prep Time: 15 minutes (Ready in 8 hours 15 minutes)

2 lb. ground turkey breast

1 cup finely chopped onions

⅛ teaspoon cloves

½ cup molasses

¼ cup cider vinegar

2 (28- to 31-oz.) cans baked beans in tomato sauce, undrained

1 (19-oz.) can cannellini beans, drained

1 (15.5- or 15-oz.) can kidney beans, drained

Chopped green onions, if desired

1. Place ground turkey in 3½- to 4-quart slow cooker; break apart with fork. Add all remaining ingredients except green onions; mix well.

2. Cover; cook on low setting for 6 to 8 hours. Sprinkle individual servings with green onions.

NUTRITION INFORMATION PER SERVING: Serving Size: ¹⁄₁₂ of Recipe • Calories 340 • Calories from Fat 10 • % Daily Value: Total Fat 1g 2% • Saturated Fat 0g 0% • Cholesterol 50mg 17% • Sodium 700mg 29% • Total Carbohydrate 53g 18% • Dietary Fiber 12g 48% • Sugars 17g • Protein 29g • Vitamin A 6% • Vitamin C 6% • Calcium 15% • Iron 20% • **DIETARY EXCHANGES:** 2½ Starch, 1 Fruit, 3 Very Lean Meat **OR** 3½ Carbohydrate, 3 Very Lean Meat

KIDS CAN HELP

Youngsters can lend a hand in the kitchen by opening up the cans of beans and even draining and pouring them into the slow cooker if you like.

southwestern turkey

YIELD: 6 SERVINGS

Prep Time: 15 minutes (Ready in 6 hours 15 minutes)

1 tablespoon olive or vegetable oil

1¼ lb. turkey breast tenderloins, cut into 1-inch pieces

1 (14.5-oz.) can diced tomatoes with Mexican seasoning, undrained

½ medium green bell pepper, thinly sliced

1 teaspoon sugar

3 teaspoons chili powder

½ teaspoon salt

2 tablespoons lime juice

1. Heat oil in large skillet over medium-high heat until hot. Add turkey; cook 4 to 6 minutes or until browned, stirring occasionally. Place turkey in 2½- to 4-quart slow cooker.

2. In small bowl, combine all remaining ingredients; mix well. Pour over turkey.

3. Cover; cook on low setting for 4 to 6 hours.

NUTRITION INFORMATION PER SERVING: Serving Size: ⅙ of Recipe • Calories 145 • Calories from Fat 25 • % Daily Value: Total Fat 3g 5% • Saturated Fat 0g 0% • Cholesterol 60mg 20% • Sodium 440mg 18% • Total Carbohydrate 7g 2% • Dietary Fiber 1g 4% • Sugars 5g • Protein 23g • Vitamin A 12% • Vitamin C 16% • Calcium 2% • Iron 8% • **DIETARY EXCHANGES:** 1 Vegetable, 3 Very Lean Meat, ½ Fat **OR** ½ Carbohydrate, 1 Vegetable, 3 Very Lean Meat, ½ Fat

MAKE IT SPECIAL

Cilantro is a popular herb used in many Southwest-style recipes. It has a pungent flavor and aroma with a cool, minty overtone. Sprinkle a couple of tablespoons of chopped fresh cilantro over the turkey just before serving to add extra flavor to this dish.

turkey drumsticks
with plum sauce

YIELD: 4 SERVINGS

Prep Time: 10 minutes (Ready in 10 hours 30 minutes)

4 turkey drumsticks (2½ to 3 lb.), skin removed

½ teaspoon salt

¼ teaspoon pepper

⅔ cup purchased plum sauce

⅓ cup sliced green onions

1 tablespoon soy sauce

1 tablespoon cold water

1 tablespoon cornstarch

1. Sprinkle turkey drumsticks with salt and pepper. Place in 5- to 6-quart slow cooker. In small bowl, combine plum sauce, onions and soy sauce; mix well. Pour over turkey.

2. Cover; cook on low setting for 8 to 10 hours.

3. About 25 minutes before serving, remove turkey from slow cooker; place on serving platter. Cover with foil to keep warm. Remove any fat from liquid in slow cooker.

4. In small bowl, blend water and cornstarch until smooth. Stir into liquid in slow cooker. Increase heat setting to high; cover and cook an additional 15 to 20 minutes or until sauce has thickened. Serve turkey with sauce.

NUTRITION INFORMATION PER SERVING: Serving Size: ¼ of Recipe • Calories 355 • Calories from Fat 70 • % Daily Value: Total Fat 8g 12% • Saturated Fat 3g 15% • Cholesterol 210mg 70% • Sodium 680mg 28% • Total Carbohydrate 17g 6% • Dietary Fiber 1g 4% • Sugars 12g • Protein 55g • Vitamin A 2% • Vitamin C 2% • Calcium 6% • Iron 28% • **DIETARY EXCHANGES:** 1 Fruit, 8 Very Lean Meat **OR** 1 Carbohydrate, 8 Very Lean Meat

DOUGHBOY TIP

Plum sauce is a sweet-and-sour sauce made from plums, apricots, sugar and seasonings. Look for it in the Asian-foods section of your grocery store. If you can't find it, feel free to substitute apricot or cherry preserves with equally delicious results.

super soups, stews and chilies

Cabbage and Pork Soup 92

Split Pea Soup with Veggies 93

Yellow Pea Soup with Chorizo 94

Hearty Steak and Tater Soup 95

Vegetable, Bean and Ham Soup 96

Cuban Black Bean Soup 97

Hamburger-Noodle Soup 98

Grandma's Chicken Noodle Soup 99

Mexicali Chicken and Corn Soup 100

Dill-Turkey Chowder 101

Turkey-Wild Rice Soup 102

Peppery Fish Chowder 103

Vegetable Minestrone Soup 104

Two-Potato Vegetable Soup 105

Creamy Butternut Squash Soup 107

French Onion Soup
with Cheesy Bread 108

Swiss Steak Stew 109

Home-Style Pork Stew 110

Curried Beef Stew 112

Hungarian Stew 113

Family-Favorite Beef Stew 114

Southwestern Chicken and
Bean Stew 115

Irish Stew 116

Chicken, Sausage and Cabbage Stew
with Wild Rice 117

Seafood Stew 119

Moroccan Chicken Stew 120

Chicken Brunswick Stew 121

Winter Vegetable Stew 122

Vegetable, Lentil and Pasta Stew 124

Ratatouille Bean Stew 125

Texas Chili 126

Chunky Beef and Pork Chili 127

Meaty Two-Bean Chili 128

Spicy Vegetarian Chili 129

TEXAS CHILI, PAGE 126

cabbage and pork soup

YIELD: 8 SERVINGS

Prep Time: 20 minutes (Ready in 8 hours 20 minutes)

1 lb. boneless country-style pork loin ribs, cut into 1-inch pieces

4 cups chopped cabbage

4 medium carrots, cut into ¼-inch slices (2 cups)

2 medium stalks celery, chopped (1 cup)

1 medium potato, peeled, cut into ½ x ¼-inch pieces

½ cup chopped onion

¼ cup firmly packed brown sugar

4 chicken-flavor bouillon cubes

4 cups water

1 (28-oz.) can crushed tomatoes, undrained

1 teaspoon crushed red pepper flakes

½ teaspoon salt

½ teaspoon pepper

1. In 4 to 5-quart slow cooker, combine all ingredients; mix well.

2. Cover; cook on low setting for about 8 hours.

NUTRITION INFORMATION PER SERVING: Serving Size: ⅛ of Recipe • Calories 190 • Calories from Fat 65 • % Daily Value: Total Fat 7g 11% • Saturated Fat 2g 10% • Cholesterol 35mg 12% • Sodium 930mg 39% • Total Carbohydrate 22g 7% • Dietary Fiber 4g 16% • Sugars 13g • Protein 14g • Vitamin A 54% • Vitamin C 28% • Calcium 8% • Iron 10% • **DIETARY EXCHANGES:** 1 Starch, 2 Vegetable, 2 Lean Meat **OR** 1 Carbohydrate, 2 Vegetable, 2 Lean Meat

DOUGHBOY TIP
Save yourself the time of chopping the cabbage, and use coleslaw blend available in the produce department. A 16-ounce bag contains about 6 cups.

split pea soup with veggies

YIELD: 8 SERVINGS

Prep Time: 15 minutes (Ready in 4 hours 50 minutes)

1 ham bone, 2 lb. ham shanks or 2 lb. smoked pork hocks

1 (16-oz.) pkg. (2¼ cups) dried split peas, sorted, rinsed

1 cup chopped onions

2 medium stalks celery, finely chopped (1 cup)

¼ teaspoon pepper

7 cups water

3 medium carrots, cut into ¼-inch slices (1½ cups)

1. In 4- to 6-quart slow cooker, combine all ingredients except carrots; stir gently to mix.

2. Cover; cook on low setting for 3 to 4 hours.

3. About 35 minutes before serving, remove ham bone from soup. Let stand about 15 minutes or until cool enough to handle.

4. Remove ham from bone. Remove excess fat from ham; cut ham into ½-inch pieces. Stir ham and carrots into soup. Increase heat setting to high; cover and cook an additional 15 minutes or until carrots are tender.

NUTRITION INFORMATION PER SERVING: Serving Size: ⅛ of Recipe • Calories 190 • Calories from Fat 45 • % Daily Value: Total Fat 5g 8% • Saturated Fat 2g 10% • Cholesterol 15mg 5% • Sodium 210mg 9% • Total Carbohydrate 33g 11% • Dietary Fiber 13g 52% • Sugars 4g • Protein 15g • Vitamin A 86% • Vitamin C 4% • Calcium 2% • Iron 12% • **DIETARY EXCHANGES:** 2 Starch, 1 Vegetable, 1 Very Lean Meat **OR** 2 Carbohydrate, 1 Vegetable, 1 Very Lean Meat

SERVE WITH

Hot grilled Cheddar cheese sandwiches are the perfect partner to this veggie soup. Add a glass of cold milk and a couple of chocolate chip cookies, and you have lunch!

yellow pea soup with chorizo

YIELD: **6** SERVINGS

Prep Time: 20 minutes (Ready in 9 hours 20 minutes)

1 (16-oz.) pkg. (2¼ cups) dried yellow split peas, sorted, rinsed

4 cups water

1 (10½-oz.) can condensed chicken broth

1 cup carrot strips (2 x ¼ x ¼ inch)

6 oz. smoked chorizo sausage, casing removed, cut into ¼-inch slices

¼ teaspoon salt

¼ teaspoon pepper

½ cup sliced green onions

1 (11-oz.) can vacuum-packed whole kernel corn with red and green peppers

1. In 4- to 6-quart slow cooker, combine all ingredients except onions and corn; stir gently to mix.

2. Cover; cook on low setting for 7 to 9 hours.

3. About 10 minutes before serving, stir onions and corn into soup. Increase heat setting to high; cover and cook an additional 5 to 10 minutes or until corn is thoroughly heated.

NUTRITION INFORMATION PER SERVING: Serving Size: ⅙ of Recipe • Calories 430 • Calories from Fat 90 • % Daily Value: Total Fat 10g 15% • Saturated Fat 3g 15% • Cholesterol 20mg 7% • Sodium 970mg 40% • Total Carbohydrate 59g 20% • Dietary Fiber 21g 84% • Sugars 7g • Protein 27g • Vitamin A 120% • Vitamin C 6% • Calcium 6% • Iron 25% • **DIETARY EXCHANGES:** 4 Starch, 2 Lean Meat **OR** 4 Carbohydrate, 2 Lean Meat

DOUGHBOY TIP

Chorizo is a coarse-ground, spicy pork sausage popular in Spanish and Mexican recipes. Be sure to remove the casing from the sausage before slicing it so it doesn't become tough during cooking.

hearty steak and tater soup

YIELD: **8 SERVINGS**

Prep Time: 20 minutes (Ready in 9 hours 55 minutes)

*1 lb. boneless beef round steak, trimmed of fat,
cut into 1¼ x 1-inch pieces*

*1 lb. small red potatoes, cut into ¼-inch slices
(4 cups)*

2 medium stalks celery, chopped (1 cup)

2 medium carrots, chopped (1 cup)

½ cup chopped onion

2 garlic cloves, minced

1 tablespoon beef-flavor instant bouillon

½ teaspoon salt

½ teaspoon pepper

4 (14-oz.) cans beef broth

1 (6-oz.) jar sliced mushrooms, undrained

½ cup water

½ cup all-purpose flour

1. In 4- to 5-quart slow cooker, combine all ingredients except water and flour; mix well.

2. Cover; cook on low setting for 8 to 9 hours.

3. About 35 minutes before serving, blend water and flour until smooth. Gradually stir into soup. Increase heat setting to high; cover and cook an additional 30 minutes or until slightly thickened.

NUTRITION INFORMATION PER SERVING: Serving Size: ⅛ of Recipe • Calories 190 • Calories from Fat 25 • % Daily Value: Total Fat 3g 5% • Saturated Fat 1g 5% • Cholesterol 30mg 10% • Sodium 1690mg 70% • Total Carbohydrate 27g 9% • Dietary Fiber 3g 12% • Sugars 3g • Protein 17g • Vitamin A 56% • Vitamin C 8% • Calcium 4% • Iron 16% • **DIETARY EXCHANGES:** 1 Starch, 2 Vegetable, 1½ Very Lean Meat **OR** 1½ Carbohydrate, 2 Vegetable, 1½ Very Lean Meat

SERVE WITH

Lumpy Cheese Bread is fun to say and fun to eat! Heat oven to 375°F. Separate a 16.3-oz. can large refrigerated flaky biscuits into 8 biscuits. Cut each biscuit into 8 pieces; place in medium bowl. Add an 8-oz. can pizza sauce and 1 cup finely shredded mozzarella cheese; toss to coat. Spread mixture in ungreased 9-inch square glass baking dish. Sprinkle with additional 1 cup finely shredded mozzarella cheese. Bake 22 to 28 minutes or until golden brown and bubbly.

vegetable, bean and ham soup

YIELD: 4 SERVINGS

Prep Time: 15 minutes (Ready in 20 hours 15 minutes)

1 cup dried navy beans, sorted, rinsed

1 cup diced cooked ham (about 6 oz.)

1 cup sliced celery

1 cup sliced carrots

2 (14-oz.) cans chicken broth

¾ cup water

¼ teaspoon garlic powder

¼ teaspoon pepper

2 bay leaves

1. Soak beans in enough water to cover for at least 8 hours or overnight.

2. Drain beans, discarding water. In 3½- to 4-quart slow cooker, combine beans and all remaining ingredients; mix well.

3. Cover; cook on low setting for 8 to 12 hours. Remove and discard bay leaves before serving.

NUTRITION INFORMATION PER SERVING: Serving Size: ¼ of Recipe • Calories 280 • Calories from Fat 35 • % Daily Value: Total Fat 4g 6% • Saturated Fat 1g 5% • Cholesterol 20mg 7% • Sodium 1300mg 54% • Total Carbohydrate 37g 12% • Dietary Fiber 14g 56% • Sugars 2g • Protein 25g • Vitamin A 170% • Vitamin C 8% • Calcium 10% • Iron 25% • **DIETARY EXCHANGES:** 2½ Starch, 2½ Very Lean Meat **OR** 2½ Carbohydrate, 2½ Very Lean Meat

DOUGHBOY TIP

Soak dried beans overnight in enough water to cover them by 2 inches. Or try the quick-soak method: Place beans in a large saucepan and add enough water to cover. Bring to a boil over high heat. Reduce heat; cover and simmer for 2 minutes. Remove saucepan from heat and let stand for 1 hour. Drain and rinse the beans thoroughly. Continue with the recipe as directed.

cuban black bean soup

YIELD: **8** SERVINGS

Prep Time: 20 minutes (Ready in 8 hours 20 minutes)

1 (16-oz.) pkg. (2⅓ cups) dried black beans, sorted, rinsed

1 cup finely chopped cooked ham

1 cup chopped onions

1 large tomato, chopped (1 cup)

1 medium green bell pepper, chopped (1 cup)

3 garlic cloves, minced

3 cups beef broth

1¾ cups water

¼ cup dark rum or apple cider

2 tablespoons oil

1½ teaspoons cumin

1½ teaspoons dried oregano leaves

1. In 3½- to 6-quart slow cooker, combine all ingredients; mix well.

2. Cover; cook on high setting for 6 to 8 hours.

NUTRITION INFORMATION PER SERVING: Serving Size: ⅛ of Recipe • Calories 265 • Calories from Fat 55 • % Daily Value: Total Fat 6g 9% • Saturated Fat 1g 5% • Cholesterol 10mg 3% • Sodium 640mg 27% • Total Carbohydrate 45g 15% • Dietary Fiber 11g 44% • Sugars 7g • Protein 19g • Vitamin A 4% • Vitamin C 16% • Calcium 12% • Iron 24% • **DIETARY EXCHANGES:** 3 Starch, 1 Very Lean Meat **OR** 3 Carbohydrate, 1 Very Lean Meat

MAKE IT SPECIAL

Top bowlfuls of this hearty soup with chopped hard-cooked eggs and chopped onions. Serve with warm flour tortillas.

hamburger-noodle soup

YIELD: 5 SERVINGS

Prep Time: 10 minutes (Ready in 8 hours 30 minutes)

1 lb. lean or extra-lean ground beef

½ cup coarsely chopped onion

1 medium stalk celery, cut into ¼-inch slices

1 (1.15-oz.) pkg. dry beefy mushroom recipe soup mix

1 (14.5-oz.) can diced tomatoes, undrained

3 cups water

2 cups frozen mixed vegetables, thawed, drained

2 oz. (1 cup) uncooked fine egg noodles

1. Brown ground beef in large skillet until thoroughly cooked, stirring frequently. Drain well.

2. In 3½- to 4-quart slow cooker, combine ground beef and all remaining ingredients except mixed vegetables and noodles; mix well.

3. Cover; cook on low setting for 6 to 8 hours.

4. About 20 minutes before serving, stir thawed vegetables and noodles into soup. Increase heat setting to high; cover and cook an additional 15 to 20 minutes or until vegetables are crisp-tender and noodles are tender.

NUTRITION INFORMATION PER SERVING: Serving Size: ⅕ of Recipe • Calories 310 • Calories from Fat 120 • % Daily Value: Total Fat 13g 20% • Saturated Fat 5g 25% • Cholesterol 65mg 22% • Sodium 700mg 29% • Total Carbohydrate 26g 9% • Dietary Fiber 4g 16% • Sugars 6g • Protein 21g • Vitamin A 25% • Vitamin C 15% • Calcium 6% • Iron 15% • **DIETARY EXCHANGES:** 1 Starch, 2 Vegetable, 2 Lean Meat, 1½ Fat **OR** 1 Carbohydrate, 2 Vegetable, 2 Lean Meat, 1½ Fat

SERVE WITH

Serve up steaming bowlfuls of this tasty soup with freshly baked refrigerated Parmesan breadsticks and a simple side of sliced pears.

grandma's chicken noodle soup

YIELD: **6** SERVINGS

Prep Time: 40 minutes (Ready in 7 hours 40 minutes)

¾ lb. boneless skinless chicken thighs, cut into 1-inch pieces

2 medium stalks celery (with leaves), sliced (1¼ cups)

1 large carrot, chopped (¾ cup)

½ cup chopped onion

1 (14.5-oz.) can diced tomatoes, undrained

1 (14-oz.) can chicken broth

1 teaspoon dried thyme leaves

1 (10-oz.) pkg. frozen sweet peas

1 cup frozen home-style egg noodles (from 12-oz. pkg.)

1. Spray large skillet with nonstick cooking spray. Heat over medium heat until hot. Add chicken; cook 5 minutes or until browned, stirring frequently.

2. In 3½- to 4-quart slow cooker, combine chicken and all remaining ingredients except peas and noodles; mix well.

3. Cover; cook on low setting for 6½ to 7 hours.

4. About 10 minutes before serving, stir peas and noodles into soup. Cover; cook on low setting for 10 minutes or until noodles are tender.

NUTRITION INFORMATION PER SERVING: Serving Size: ⅙ of Recipe • Calories 215 • Calories from Fat 65 • % Daily Value: Total Fat 7g 11% • Saturated Fat 2g 10% • Cholesterol 45mg 15% • Sodium 1260mg 53% • Total Carbohydrate 20g 7% • Dietary Fiber 4g 16% • Sugars 5g • Protein 22g • Vitamin A 22% • Vitamin C 14% • Calcium 6% • Iron 18% • **DIETARY EXCHANGES:** 1 Starch, 1 Vegetable, 2 Very Lean Meat, 1 Fat **OR** 1 Carbohydrate, 1 Vegetable, 2 Very Lean Meat, 1 Fat

DOUGHBOY TIP

The home-style noodles add a home-cooked flavor to this family-favorite soup, but if they're not available, you can use a cup of uncooked fine egg noodles.

mexicali chicken and corn soup

YIELD: 6 SERVINGS

Prep Time: 10 minutes (Ready in 12 hours 30 minutes)

1 lb. boneless skinless chicken thighs, cut into 1-inch pieces

1 (1-lb.) pkg. frozen whole kernel corn

2 (14-oz.) cans chicken broth

1 (14.5-oz.) can Mexican-style stewed tomatoes, undrained

¾ cup uncooked instant brown rice

1 (1.25-oz.) pkg. taco seasoning mix

1. In 3½- to 4-quart slow cooker, combine chicken, corn, broth and tomatoes; mix well.

2. Cover; cook on low setting for 8 to 12 hours.

3. About 20 minutes before serving, stir rice and taco seasoning mix into soup. Increase heat setting to high; cover and cook an additional 20 minutes or until rice is tender. Stir soup before serving.

NUTRITION INFORMATION PER SERVING: Serving Size: ⅙ of Recipe • Calories 270 • Calories from Fat 60 • % Daily Value: Total Fat 7g 11% • Saturated Fat 2g 10% • Cholesterol 50mg 17% • Sodium 1060mg 44% • Total Carbohydrate 32g 11% • Dietary Fiber 3g 12% • Sugars 5g • Protein 19g • Vitamin A 10% • Vitamin C 15% • Calcium 4% • Iron 10% • **DIETARY EXCHANGES:** 2 Starch, 2 Lean Meat **OR** 2 Carbohydrate, 2 Lean Meat

SERVE WITH

Accompany this Mexican soup with warm flour tortillas and a cool salad made with avocado and orange slices. Tall glasses of lemonade or limeade are the ultimate thirst quencher.

dill-turkey chowder

YIELD: 6 SERVINGS

Prep Time: 15 minutes (Ready in 8 hours 35 minutes)

1 lb. uncooked turkey breast slices, cut into 1-inch pieces

¾ teaspoon garlic-pepper blend

½ teaspoon salt

6 to 8 small red potatoes, cut into 1-inch pieces

½ cup chopped onion

2 medium carrots, sliced (1 cup)

2 teaspoons dried dill weed

2½ cups chicken broth

1 (15.25-oz.) can whole kernel corn, drained

1 cup half-and-half

3 tablespoons cornstarch

1. Place turkey in 4- to 5-quart slow cooker; sprinkle with garlic-pepper blend and salt. Add all remaining ingredients except half-and-half and cornstarch; mix well.

2. Cover; cook on low setting for 6 to 8 hours.

3. About 25 minutes before serving, in small bowl, blend half-and-half and cornstarch until smooth. Gradually stir into chowder. Increase heat setting to high; cover and cook an additional 20 minutes until thickened, stirring occasionally.

NUTRITION INFORMATION PER SERVING: Serving Size: ⅙ of Recipe • Calories 265 • Calories from Fat 65 • % Daily Value: Total Fat 7g 11% • Saturated Fat 3g 15% • Cholesterol 65mg 22% • Sodium 840mg 35% • Total Carbohydrate 33g 11% • Dietary Fiber 3g 12% • Sugars 6g • Protein 21g • Vitamin A 36% • Vitamin C 12% • Calcium 8% • Iron 14% • **DIETARY EXCHANGES:** 2 Starch, 1 Vegetable, 1½ Very Lean Meat **OR** 2 Carbohydrate, 1 Vegetable, 1½ Very Lean Meat

KIDS CAN HELP

Kids can help mix the cornstarch with the liquid by using a jar. Screw the lid on tight, and shake the jar until the mixture is smooth.

turkey-wild rice soup

YIELD: 6 SERVINGS

Prep Time: 20 minutes (Ready in 8 hours 40 minutes)

2 teaspoons oil

1/2 cup chopped onion

2 medium stalks celery, diced (1 cup)

2 medium carrots, diced (1 cup)

1 cup diced smoked turkey (about 6 oz.)

1/2 cup uncooked wild rice

1 teaspoon dried tarragon leaves

1/4 teaspoon pepper

2 (14-oz.) cans chicken broth

1 (12-oz.) can evaporated fat-free milk

1/3 cup all-purpose flour

1 cup frozen sweet peas, thawed

2 tablespoons dry sherry, if desired

1. Heat oil in large skillet over medium heat until hot. Add onion; cook about 4 minutes or until tender, stirring occasionally.

2. In 3½- to 6-quart slow cooker, combine onion, celery, carrots, turkey, wild rice, tarragon and pepper; mix well. Pour broth over top.

3. Cover; cook on low setting for 6 to 8 hours.

4. About 25 minutes before serving, in small bowl, blend milk and flour until smooth. Gradually stir into soup. Add peas and sherry; mix well. Cover; cook on low setting an additional 20 minutes or until sauce has thickened.

NUTRITION INFORMATION PER SERVING: Serving Size: 1/6 of Recipe • Calories 245 • Calories from Fat 65 • % Daily Value: Total Fat 7g 11% • Saturated Fat 2g 10% • Cholesterol 30mg 10% • Sodium 750mg 31% • Total Carbohydrate 31g 10% • Dietary Fiber 3g 12% • Sugars 10g • Protein 18g • Vitamin A 80% • Vitamin C 6% • Calcium 20% • Iron 10% • **DIETARY EXCHANGES:** 1 Starch, 3 Vegetable, 1 Lean Meat, 1 Fat **OR** 2 Carbohydrate, 3 Vegetable, 1 Lean Meat, 1 Fat

MAKE IT SPECIAL

Perk up the presentation of this rich and creamy soup by garnishing each serving with toasted sliced or slivered almonds and chopped fresh parsley.

peppery fish chowder

YIELD: **6 SERVINGS**

Prep Time: 15 minutes (Ready in 10 hours)

2 medium stalks celery, chopped (1 cup)	1 tablespoon Worcestershire sauce
1 medium bell pepper, chopped (1 cup)	1 teaspoon salt
½ cup chopped onion	¼ teaspoon ground red pepper (cayenne)
2 garlic cloves, minced	1 lb. firm-fleshed fish steak, cut into 1-inch pieces
2 (14.5-oz.) cans diced tomatoes, undrained	½ cup uncooked instant white rice
2 cups vegetable juice cocktail	3 tablespoons chopped fresh parsley
1 cup dry white wine or vegetable broth	

1. In 3½- to 6-quart slow cooker, combine celery, bell pepper, onion, garlic, tomatoes, vegetable juice cocktail, wine, Worcestershire sauce, salt and ground red pepper; mix well.

2. Cover; cook on low setting for 7 to 9 hours or on high setting for 3 to 4 hours.

3. About 45 minutes before serving, stir fish, rice and parsley into chowder. Increase heat setting to high; cover and cook an additional 30 to 45 minutes or until fish flakes easily with fork.

NUTRITION INFORMATION PER SERVING: Serving Size: ⅙ of Recipe • Calories 155 • Calories from Fat 10 • % Daily Value: Total Fat 1g 2% • Saturated Fat 0g 0% • Cholesterol 40mg 13% • Sodium 1000mg 42% • Total Carbohydrate 22g 7% • Dietary Fiber 3g 12% • Sugars 8g • Protein 17g • Vitamin A 40% • Vitamin C 54% • Calcium 8% • Iron 12% • **DIETARY EXCHANGES:** 1 Starch, 1 Vegetable, 1½ Very Lean Meat **OR** 1 Carbohydrate, 1 Vegetable, 1½ Very Lean Meat

DOUGHBOY TIP
Any firm-fleshed fish, such as halibut, haddock, swordfish, pollock, tuna or red snapper, works well in this soup.

vegetable minestrone soup

YIELD: 6 SERVINGS
Prep Time: 15 minutes (Ready in 10 hours 35 minutes)

2 medium carrots, cut into ½-inch slices (1 cup)

1 medium stalk celery, coarsely chopped (½ cup)

1 medium onion, halved crosswise, cut into thin wedges

1 garlic clove, minced

2 (14-oz.) cans chicken broth

1 (19-oz.) can cannellini beans, drained, rinsed

1 (15.5- or 15-oz.) can kidney beans, drained, rinsed

1 (14.5-oz.) can Italian-style stewed tomatoes, undrained, cut up

½ teaspoon salt

⅛ teaspoon pepper

1 cup frozen cut leaf spinach, thawed

3 oz. uncooked spaghetti, broken into thirds (¾ cup)

1. In 3½- or 4-quart slow cooker, combine all ingredients except spinach and spaghetti; mix well.

2. Cover; cook on low setting for 7 to 10 hours.

3. About 20 minutes before serving, stir thawed spinach and spaghetti into soup. Increase heat setting to high; cover and cook an additional 15 to 20 minutes or until spaghetti is tender.

NUTRITION INFORMATION PER SERVING: Serving Size: ⅙ of Recipe • Calories 240 • Calories from Fat 20 • % Daily Value: Total Fat 2g 3% • Saturated Fat 0g 0% • Cholesterol 0mg 0% • Sodium 970mg 40% • Total Carbohydrate 43g 14% • Dietary Fiber 9g 36% • Sugars 5g • Protein 13g • Vitamin A 160% • Vitamin C 15% • Calcium 10% • Iron 20% • **DIETARY EXCHANGES:** 2½ Starch, 1 Vegetable, ½ Very Lean Meat **OR** 2½ Carbohydrate, 1 Vegetable, ½ Very Lean Meat

MAKE IT SPECIAL
For an attractive touch that also adds flavor, garnish individual bowls of this soup with shredded fresh Parmesan cheese, chopped fresh parsley or swirls of basil pesto.

two-potato vegetable soup

YIELD: 5 SERVINGS
Prep Time: 10 minutes (Ready in 12 hours 25 minutes)

1 medium russet or baking potato, cut into ½-inch cubes (about 1 cup)

1 medium dark-orange sweet potato, peeled, cut into ½-inch cubes (1¼ cups)

¼ cup chopped onion

1 (14.5-oz.) can diced tomatoes with basil, garlic and oregano, undrained

2½ cups water

¾ teaspoon salt

2 vegetarian vegetable bouillon cubes

1 (10-oz.) pkg. (about 2 cups) frozen peas and carrots

1. In 3½- to 4-quart slow cooker, combine all ingredients except peas and carrots; mix well.

2. Cover; cook on low setting for 8 to 12 hours.

3. About 15 minutes before serving, stir peas and carrots into soup. Cover; cook an additional 15 minutes or until peas and carrots are thoroughly heated.

NUTRITION INFORMATION PER SERVING: Serving Size: ⅕ of Recipe • Calories 120 • Calories from Fat 10 • % Daily Value: Total Fat 1g 2% • Saturated Fat 0g 0% • Cholesterol 0mg 0% • Sodium 1030mg 43% • Total Carbohydrate 23g 8% • Dietary Fiber 4g 16% • Sugars 7g • Protein 4g • Vitamin A 220% • Vitamin C 30% • Calcium 6% • Iron 8% • **DIETARY EXCHANGES:** 1½ Starch OR 1½ Carbohydrate

SERVE WITH

Nothing tastes better than a bowl of soup with **Ham 'n' Cheese Biscuit Sandwiches.** Bake a 16.3-oz. can large refrigerated buttermilk biscuits as directed on can. Split each warm biscuit. Place 2 slices fully cooked ham and 1 slice American cheese on each bottom half of biscuit. Top with remaining biscuit halves.

creamy butternut squash soup

YIELD: 6 SERVINGS

Prep Time: 20 minutes (Ready in 8 hours 50 minutes)

2 tablespoons margarine or butter

1/2 cup chopped onion

1 (2-lb.) butternut squash, peeled, cubed

2 cups water

1/2 teaspoon dried marjoram leaves

1/4 teaspoon coarsely ground black pepper

1/8 teaspoon ground red pepper (cayenne)

4 chicken-flavor bouillon cubes

1 (8-oz.) pkg. cream cheese, cubed

1. Melt margarine in large skillet over medium heat. Add onion; cook until crisp-tender, stirring occasionally.

2. In 3 1/2- to 4-quart slow cooker, combine onion and all remaining ingredients except cream cheese; mix well.

3. Cover; cook on low setting for 6 to 8 hours.

4. About 40 minutes before serving, place about 1/3 of mixture at a time into blender container or food processor bowl with metal blade. Cover; blend or process on high speed until smooth. Return mixture to slow cooker.

5. Stir in cream cheese. Cover; cook on low setting an additional 25 to 30 minutes or until cheese is melted, stirring with wire whisk until smooth.

NUTRITION INFORMATION PER SERVING: Serving Size: 1/6 of Recipe • Calories 235 • Calories from Fat 155 • % Daily Value: Total Fat 17g 26% • Saturated Fat 9g 45% • Cholesterol 40mg 13% • Sodium 940mg 39% • Total Carbohydrate 17g 6% • Dietary Fiber 2g 8% • Sugars 7g • Protein 5g • Vitamin A 100% • Vitamin C 16% • Calcium 8% • Iron 6% • **DIETARY EXCHANGES:** 3 Vegetable, 3 1/2 Fat **OR** 1 Carbohydrate, 3 Vegetable, 3 1/2 Fat

MAKE IT SPECIAL

For a chunky veggie version of this soup, stir in a 1-pound package of frozen mixed vegetables (thawed and drained) with the cream cheese.

french onion soup with cheesy bread

YIELD: 8 SERVINGS

Prep Time: 25 minutes (Ready in 10 hours)

3 large onions, sliced (3 cups)

3 tablespoons margarine or butter, melted

3 tablespoons all-purpose flour

1 teaspoon sugar

¼ teaspoon pepper

1 tablespoon Worcestershire sauce

4 (14-oz.) cans beef broth

8 (1-inch-thick) slices French bread

3 oz. (¾ cup) shredded mozzarella cheese

2 tablespoons grated or shredded fresh Parmesan cheese

1. In 3½- to 6-quart slow cooker, combine onions and margarine. Cover; cook on high setting for 30 to 35 minutes or until onions begin to slightly brown around edges.

2. In small bowl, blend flour, sugar, pepper and Worcestershire sauce until smooth. Stir flour mixture and broth into onions.

3. Cover; cook on low setting for 7 to 9 hours or on high setting for 3 to 4 hours.

4. About 10 minutes before serving, place bread slices on broiler pan. Sprinkle with mozzarella and Parmesan cheeses. Broil 5 to 6 inches from heat for about 3 minutes or until cheese is melted. Top individual servings of soup with 1 slice cheesy bread.

NUTRITION INFORMATION PER SERVING: Serving Size: ⅛ of Recipe • Calories 180 • Calories from Fat 70 • % Daily Value: Total Fat 8g 12% • Saturated Fat 5g 25% • Cholesterol 20mg 7% • Sodium 750mg 31% • Total Carbohydrate 21g 7% • Dietary Fiber 2g 8% • Sugars 4g • Protein 8g • Vitamin A 6% • Vitamin C 2% • Calcium 14% • Iron 6% • **DIETARY EXCHANGES:** 1 Starch, 1 Vegetable, 1½ Fat **OR** 1 Carbohydrate, 1 Vegetable, 1½ Fat

DOUGHBOY TIP

If you don't have the 14-oz. cans of broth on hand, you can use three 10½-oz. cans of condensed beef broth with 2½ soup cans of water. Or add 7 cups water with 7 beef-flavor bouillon cubes or 2 heaping tablespoons of beef-flavor instant bouillon.

swiss steak stew

YIELD: 6 SERVINGS

Prep Time: 20 minutes (Ready in 8 hours 50 minutes)

¼ cup all-purpose flour

½ teaspoon seasoned salt

1½ lb. boneless beef round steak, trimmed of fat, cut into 6 pieces

1 (14.5-oz.) can diced tomatoes with basil, garlic and oregano, undrained

¾ cup water

3 cups quartered unpeeled small red potatoes

1 large onion, halved lengthwise, thinly sliced

1 medium green bell pepper, cut into strips

1 cup frozen whole kernel corn

Salt and pepper

1. In medium bowl, combine flour and seasoned salt; mix well. Add beef pieces; turn to coat.

2. Spray large nonstick skillet with nonstick cooking spray. Heat over medium-high heat until hot. Add beef; cook 5 to 6 minutes or until browned on both sides, turning once.

3. Meanwhile, add tomatoes and water to any remaining flour mixture; mix well.

4. In 3½- to 4-quart slow cooker, layer potatoes, browned beef, onion and bell pepper. Pour tomato mixture over top.

5. Cover; cook on low setting for 7 to 8 hours.

6. About 30 minutes before serving, stir corn into stew. Cover; cook on low setting an additional 20 to 30 minutes or until corn is tender. If desired, add salt and pepper to taste.

NUTRITION INFORMATION PER SERVING: Serving Size: ⅙ of Recipe • Calories 255 • Calories from Fat 35 • % Daily Value: Total Fat 4g 6% • Saturated Fat 1g 5% • Cholesterol 60mg 20% • Sodium 350mg 15% • Total Carbohydrate 33g 11% • Dietary Fiber 4g 16% • Sugars 6g • Protein 26g • Vitamin A 6% • Vitamin C 30% • Calcium 4% • Iron 20% • **DIETARY EXCHANGES:** 2 Starch, 1 Vegetable, 2 Very Lean Meat **OR** 2 Carbohydrate, 1 Vegetable, 2 Very Lean Meat

DOUGHBOY TIP

Either top or bottom round steak will work in this recipe. If the steak has a bone, purchase about 2 pounds. Carefully cut out and discard the bone before cooking.

home-style pork stew

Prep Time: 15 minutes (Ready in 8 hours 35 minutes)

1 tablespoon oil

1 (1½-lb.) boneless pork shoulder roast, cut into 1½-inch pieces

⅛ teaspoon salt

⅛ teaspoon pepper

8 small red potatoes, unpeeled, quartered

2 cups fresh baby carrots, cut in half lengthwise

1 (12-oz.) jar pork gravy

¼ cup ketchup

½ teaspoon dried rosemary leaves

¼ teaspoon pepper

⅛ teaspoon ground sage

1½ cups frozen cut green beans, thawed

1. Heat oil in large skillet over high heat until hot. Add pork; sprinkle with salt and ⅛ teaspoon pepper. Cook 3 to 5 minutes or until browned, stirring frequently.

2. In 4- to 6-quart slow cooker, combine pork and all remaining ingredients except green beans.

3. Cover; cook on low setting for 6 to 8 hours.

4. About 20 minutes before serving, stir green beans into stew. Increase heat setting to high; cover and cook an additional 15 to 20 minutes or until beans are tender.

NUTRITION INFORMATION PER SERVING: Serving Size: ⅙ of Recipe • Calories 380 • Calories from Fat 110 • % Daily Value: Total Fat 12g 18% • Saturated Fat 3g 15% • Cholesterol 50mg 17% • Sodium 530mg 22% • Total Carbohydrate 47g 16% • Dietary Fiber 5g 20% • Sugars 6g • Protein 20g • Vitamin A 220% • Vitamin C 30% • Calcium 6% • Iron 20% • **DIETARY EXCHANGES:** 3 Starch, 1 Vegetable, 1½ Lean Meat, 1 Fat **OR** 3 Carbohydrate, 1 Vegetable, 1½ Lean Meat, 1 Fat

SERVE WITH
Make a stick-to-your-ribs dinner with this home-cooked stew and a batch of hot refrigerated biscuits. Preheat the oven and bake the biscuits after you've added the green beans to the stew.

curried beef stew

Prep Time: 15 minutes (Ready in 10 hours 15 minutes)

1 cup small whole onions, peeled

1 cup fresh baby carrots

12 small new potatoes, cut in half (about 4 cups)

2 lb. boneless beef chuck steak, trimmed of fat, cut into 1½-inch pieces

1 (14.5-oz.) can diced tomatoes, undrained

½ cup apple juice

4 teaspoons curry powder

½ teaspoon salt

¼ teaspoon pepper

1. In 3½- to 4-quart slow cooker, layer onions, carrots and potatoes. Place beef over vegetables.

2. In medium bowl, combine all remaining ingredients; mix well. Pour over beef.

3. Cover; cook on low setting for 8 to 10 hours.

NUTRITION INFORMATION PER SERVING: Serving Size: ⅙ of Recipe • Calories 405 • Calories from Fat 160 • % Daily Value: Total Fat 18g 28% • Saturated Fat 7g 35% • Cholesterol 95mg 32% • Sodium 390mg 16% • Total Carbohydrate 31g 10% • Dietary Fiber 4g 16% • Sugars 7g • Protein 34g • Vitamin A 100% • Vitamin C 20% • Calcium 6% • Iron 30% • **DIETARY EXCHANGES:** 2 Starch, 4 Lean Meat, 1 Fat **OR** 2 Carbohydrate, 4 Lean Meat, 1 Fat

SERVE WITH

To make a hearty meal out of this thick and yummy stew, serve it with warmed pita bread and a cup of steaming-hot tea.

hungarian stew

YIELD: 8 SERVINGS

Prep Time: 15 minutes (Ready in 8 hours 45 minutes)

1 (2-lb.) lean boneless beef chuck roast, cut into ¾-inch pieces

2 cups fresh baby carrots

1 medium onion, sliced

1 medium green bell pepper, sliced

⅓ cup all-purpose flour

3 teaspoons paprika

½ teaspoon salt

½ teaspoon dried thyme leaves

¼ teaspoon pepper

½ cup chili sauce

1 (14-oz.) can beef broth

2 cups sliced fresh mushrooms

1 (16-oz.) pkg. (10 cups) uncooked wide egg noodles

1 (8-oz.) container sour cream

2 tablespoons chopped fresh parsley

1. In 3½- to 4-quart slow cooker, combine beef, carrots, onion and bell pepper. Add flour, paprika, salt, thyme and pepper; toss to coat. Add chili sauce and broth; mix well.

2. Cover; cook on low setting for 7 to 8 hours.

3. About 35 minutes before serving, stir mushrooms into stew. Cover; cook on low setting an additional 20 to 30 minutes or until mushrooms are tender. Meanwhile, cook noodles to desired doneness as directed on package. Drain.

4. At serving time, stir sour cream into stew until well mixed. Spoon noodles into individual shallow bowls. Top each with stew. Sprinkle with parsley.

NUTRITION INFORMATION PER SERVING: Serving Size: ⅛ of Recipe • Calories 480 • Calories from Fat 130 • % Daily Value: Total Fat 14g 22% • Saturated Fat 6g 30% • Cholesterol 130mg 43% • Sodium 610mg 25% • Total Carbohydrate 56g 19% • Dietary Fiber 4g 16% • Sugars 9g • Protein 32g • Vitamin A 180% • Vitamin C 20% • Calcium 8% • Iron 35% • **DIETARY EXCHANGES:** 3 Starch, 1 Vegetable, 3 Lean Meat, 1 Fat **OR** 3 Carbohydrate, 1 Vegetable, 3 Lean Meat, 1 Fat

DOUGHBOY TIP
A terrific time-saver is to cut up the veggies and meat for this stew the night before. Place them in separate containers, cover tightly and refrigerate until you are ready to begin.

family-favorite beef stew

YIELD: 6 SERVINGS

Prep Time: 25 minutes (Ready in 10 hours 25 minutes)

1½ lb. beef stew meat, cut into ¾-inch cubes	1½ cups frozen pearl onions (from 16-oz. pkg.)
5 tablespoons all-purpose flour	1 (1-lb.) pkg. fresh baby carrots
1 teaspoon salt	1 (12-oz.) jar beef gravy
½ teaspoon pepper	1 (14.5-oz.) can diced tomatoes, undrained
1 tablespoon oil	¼ cup cold water
1 lb. small (2½- to 3-inch) red potatoes, quartered	

1. On waxed paper, sprinkle beef with 2 tablespoons of the flour, salt and pepper; toss to coat. Heat oil in large skillet over medium-high heat until hot. Add coated beef; cook and stir 4 to 6 minutes or until browned, stirring occasionally.

2. In 4- to 6-quart slow cooker, layer potatoes, onions and carrots. Add browned beef; sprinkle with any remaining flour mixture. Top with gravy and tomatoes.

3. Cover; cook on low setting for 8 to 10 hours.

4. About 10 minutes before serving, blend water and remaining 3 tablespoons flour until smooth. Stir into stew. Increase heat setting to high; cover and cook an additional 10 minutes or until thickened.

NUTRITION INFORMATION PER SERVING: Serving Size: ⅙ of Recipe • Calories 380 • Calories from Fat 90 • % Daily Value: Total Fat 10g 15% • Saturated Fat 3g 15% • Cholesterol 80mg 27% • Sodium 910mg 38% • Total Carbohydrate 41g 14% • Dietary Fiber 6g 24% • Sugars 10g • Protein 31g • Vitamin A 430% • Vitamin C 30% • Calcium 8% • Iron 30% • **DIETARY EXCHANGES:** 1½ Starch, ½ Fruit, 2 Vegetable, 3 Lean Meat **OR** 2 Carbohydrate, 2 Vegetable, 3 Lean Meat

DOUGHBOY TIP
Two medium onions, peeled and cut into thin wedges, can be used in place of the frozen pearl onions.

southwestern chicken and bean stew

YIELD: 6 SERVINGS

Prep Time: 20 minutes (Ready in 20 hours 20 minutes)

1 cup dried pinto beans, sorted, rinsed

2 lb. cut-up frying chicken, skin removed

1 cup frozen whole kernel corn

1 cup chunky-style salsa

1 (14-oz.) can chicken broth

1 (4.5-oz.) can chopped green chiles

1 teaspoon cumin

2 tablespoons chopped fresh cilantro

1. Soak beans in enough water to cover for at least 8 hours or overnight.

2. Drain beans, discarding water. In 3½- to 4-quart slow cooker, combine beans and all remaining ingredients except cilantro; mix well.

3. Cover; cook on low setting for 10 to 12 hours.

4. With slotted spoon, remove chicken from slow cooker. Remove chicken from bones; discard bones. Cut chicken into pieces; return chicken to stew. Stir in cilantro.

NUTRITION INFORMATION PER SERVING: Serving Size: ⅙ of Recipe • Calories 250 • Calories from Fat 45 • % Daily Value: Total Fat 5g 8% • Saturated Fat 1g 5% • Cholesterol 45mg 15% • Sodium 650mg 27% • Total Carbohydrate 29g 10% • Dietary Fiber 9g 36% • Sugars 3g • Protein 23g • Vitamin A 4% • Vitamin C 10% • Calcium 8% • Iron 15% • **DIETARY EXCHANGES:** 2 Starch, 2½ Very Lean Meat **OR** 2 Carbohydrate, 2½ Very Lean Meat

DOUGHBOY TIP

A quick way to kick up the spice in this recipe is to use a can of "hot" green chiles. Check the label on the can to see how hot or mild the chiles are.

irish stew

YIELD: 8 SERVINGS

Prep Time: 15 minutes (Ready in 10 hours 15 minutes)

2 lb. lean lamb stew meat

6 medium potatoes (2 lb.), cut into ½-inch slices

3 medium onions, sliced

1 teaspoon salt

¼ teaspoon pepper

1 teaspoon dried thyme leaves

1 (14-oz.) can beef broth

Chopped fresh parsley, if desired

1. In 3½- to 6-quart slow cooker, layer half each of the lamb, potatoes and onions. Sprinkle with half each of the salt, pepper and thyme. Repeat layers and sprinkle with remaining seasonings. Pour broth over top.

2. Cover; cook on low setting for 8 to 10 hours or on high setting for 3 to 5 hours. Sprinkle individual servings of stew with parsley.

NUTRITION INFORMATION PER SERVING: Serving Size: ⅛ of Recipe • Calories 240 • Calories from Fat 65 • % Daily Value: Total Fat 7g 11% • Saturated Fat 2g 10% • Cholesterol 60mg 20% • Sodium 580mg 24% • Total Carbohydrate 25g 8% • Dietary Fiber 3g 12% • Sugars 3g • Protein 22g • Vitamin A 0% • Vitamin C 10% • Calcium 2% • Iron 16% • **DIETARY EXCHANGES:** 1 Starch, 2 Vegetable, 2 Lean Meat **OR** 1 Carbohydrate, 2 Vegetable, 2 Lean Meat

DOUGHBOY TIP
If your family doesn't care for the flavor of lamb, you can substitute 2 pounds of lean beef stew meat.

chicken, sausage and cabbage stew with wild rice

YIELD: 8 SERVINGS

Prep Time: 20 minutes (Ready in 8 hours 20 minutes)

2 cups coarsely chopped (1-inch pieces) cabbage

1 cup fresh baby carrots, quartered lengthwise

1 cup uncooked wild rice, rinsed

½ cup chopped onion

2 garlic cloves, minced

1 (8-oz.) pkg. (3 cups) sliced fresh mushrooms

1 lb. boneless skinless chicken thighs, cut into 1½-inch pieces

½ lb. (about 2) mild Italian pork sausage links, cut into 1-inch pieces

2 (14-oz.) cans chicken broth

1 (10¾-oz.) can condensed cream of mushroom soup

1. In 3½- to 4-quart slow cooker, combine all ingredients except broth and soup; mix well.

2. In medium bowl, combine broth and soup; blend well. Pour over meat and vegetables in slow cooker; stir gently to combine.

3. Cover; cook on low setting for 6 to 8 hours.

NUTRITION INFORMATION PER SERVING: Serving Size: ⅛ of Recipe • Calories 290 • Calories from Fat 120 • % Daily Value: Total Fat 13g 20% • Saturated Fat 4g 20% • Cholesterol 55mg 18% • Sodium 830mg 35% • Total Carbohydrate 23g 8% • Dietary Fiber 3g 12% • Sugars 4g • Protein 21g • Vitamin A 80% • Vitamin C 10% • Calcium 4% • Iron 10% • **DIETARY EXCHANGES:** 1 Starch, 1 Vegetable, 2½ Lean Meat, 1 Fat **OR** 1 Carbohydrate, 1 Vegetable, 2½ Lean Meat, 1 Fat

SERVE WITH

Serve **Cheddar Cheese Pull-Apart** with this hearty stew. Heat oven to 400°F. Line an 8-inch round cake pan with foil; spray generously with nonstick cooking spray. Mix 1 cup shredded Cheddar cheese and ½ teaspoon garlic powder. Separate a 12-oz. can refrigerated buttermilk flaky biscuits into 10 biscuits; cut each into quarters. Layer half in the pan and sprinkle with half the cheese; repeat. Bake 20 to 26 minutes or until golden brown. Lift biscuits from pan using foil. Cool 5 minutes; remove foil.

seafood stew

YIELD: 8 SERVINGS
Prep Time: 20 minutes (Ready in 5 hours 5 minutes)

2 cups chopped onions

2 medium stalks celery, finely chopped (1 cup)

5 garlic cloves, minced

1 (28-oz.) can diced tomatoes, undrained

1 (8-oz.) bottle clam juice

1 (6-oz.) can tomato paste

½ cup dry white wine or water

1 tablespoon red wine vinegar

1 tablespoon olive or vegetable oil

2½ teaspoons dried Italian seasoning

¼ teaspoon sugar

¼ teaspoon crushed red pepper flakes

1 bay leaf

1 lb. firm-fleshed white fish, cut into 1-inch pieces

¾ lb. shelled deveined uncooked medium shrimp

1 (6½-oz.) can chopped clams with juice, undrained

1 (6-oz.) can crabmeat, drained

¼ cup chopped fresh parsley

1. In 5- to 6-quart slow cooker, combine onions, celery, garlic, tomatoes, clam juice, tomato paste, wine, vinegar, oil, Italian seasoning, sugar, pepper flakes and bay leaf; mix well.

2. Cover; cook on high setting for 3 to 4 hours.

3. About 45 minutes before serving, stir fish, shrimp, clams with juice and crabmeat into stew. Reduce heat setting to low; cover and cook an additional 30 to 45 minutes or until fish flakes easily with fork. Remove and discard bay leaf. Stir in parsley.

NUTRITION INFORMATION PER SERVING: Serving Size: ⅛ of Recipe • Calories 200 • Calories from Fat 35 • % Daily Value: Total Fat 4g 6% • Saturated Fat 1g 5% • Cholesterol 125mg 42% • Sodium 600mg 25% • Total Carbohydrate 14g 5% • Dietary Fiber 3g 12% • Sugars 5g • Protein 30g • Vitamin A 24% • Vitamin C 28% • Calcium 12% • Iron 50% • **DIETARY EXCHANGES:** 3 Vegetable, 3½ Very Lean Meat

SERVE WITH

Pass a basket of warm **Cheesy Dill Crescents** to complement the seafood stew. Separate an 8-oz. can refrigerated crescent dinner rolls into 8 triangles. Mix 1 tablespoon softened margarine, 2 tablespoons grated Parmesan cheese and 1 teaspoon dried dill weed. Brush mixture over each triangle. Roll and bake as directed on can.

moroccan chicken stew

YIELD: 6 SERVINGS

Prep Time: 20 minutes (Ready in 10 hours 45 minutes)

STEW

2 turnips, peeled, cut into 1-inch pieces
(about 1¼ cups)

1 cup fresh baby carrots, halved lengthwise

½ cup chopped onion

1 tablespoon chicken-flavor instant bouillon and
seasoning

1½ teaspoons cumin

¼ teaspoon cinnamon

¼ teaspoon ground red pepper (cayenne)

6 boneless skinless chicken thighs (about 1¼ lb.)

1½ cups water

3 tablespoons lemon juice

1 small zucchini (about 4 oz.),
cut into ½-inch pieces

1 small yellow summer squash (about 4 oz.),
cut into ½-inch pieces

1 (15-oz.) can garbanzo beans or chickpeas,
drained

COUSCOUS

1 (10-oz.) pkg. uncooked couscous

2 cups water

1 tablespoon olive or vegetable oil

½ teaspoon salt

1. In 3½- to 4-quart slow cooker, combine turnips, carrots and onion. In small bowl, combine bouillon, cumin, cinnamon and ground red pepper; mix well. Sprinkle over vegetables.

2. Top vegetables with chicken thighs. Pour 1½ cups water and lemon juice over chicken.

3. Cover; cook on low setting for 8 to 10 hours.

4. About 30 minutes before serving, gently stir zucchini, summer squash and garbanzo beans into stew. Meanwhile, during last 5 minutes of cooking, prepare couscous as directed on package using 2 cups water, oil and salt. Spoon couscous into individual shallow bowls. Top each with stew.

NUTRITION INFORMATION PER SERVING: Serving Size: ⅙ of Recipe • Calories 420 • Calories from Fat 100 • % Daily Value: Total Fat 11g 17% • Saturated Fat 3g 15% • Cholesterol 60mg 20% • Sodium 850mg 35% • Total Carbohydrate 54g 18% • Dietary Fiber 8g 32% • Sugars 5g • Protein 27g • Vitamin A 110% • Vitamin C 15% • Calcium 8% • Iron 15% • **DIETARY EXCHANGES:** 3½ Starch, 1 Vegetable, 2 Lean Meat, ½ Fat **OR** 3½ Carbohydrate, 1 Vegetable, 2 Lean Meat, ½ Fat

SERVE WITH

Need a quick and easy dessert? **Chocolate-Filled Crescents** are the answer. Separate a 15.5-oz. can large refrigerated crescent dinner rolls into 6 triangles. Place a heaping teaspoon of chocolate chips on wide end of each triangle. Roll and bake as directed on can.

chicken brunswick stew

YIELD: 6 SERVINGS

Prep Time: 15 minutes (Ready in 8 hours 45 minutes)

2 tablespoons all-purpose flour

2 teaspoons chicken-flavor instant bouillon and seasoning

1½ teaspoons poultry seasoning

⅛ teaspoon pepper

6 bone-in chicken thighs (about 1½ lb.), skin removed

2 medium Yukon Gold potatoes (about 1 lb.), cut into 1-inch pieces (about 3 cups)

½ cup chopped onion

1 (15-oz.) can tomato sauce

1 tablespoon Worcestershire sauce

1 (9-oz.) pkg. frozen baby lima beans in a pouch, thawed

1 (9-oz.) pkg. frozen whole kernel corn in a pouch, thawed

Salt and pepper

1. In large resealable food storage plastic bag, combine flour, bouillon, poultry seasoning and pepper; mix well. Add chicken thighs, potatoes and onion; seal bag and shake to coat. Place chicken and vegetables in 3½- to 4-quart slow cooker.

2. In small bowl, combine tomato sauce and Worcestershire sauce; mix well. Pour over chicken and vegetables; stir gently to combine.

3. Cover; cook on low setting for 6 to 8 hours.

4. About 35 minutes before serving, stir lima beans and corn into stew. Cover; cook on low setting an additional 30 minutes or until beans and corn are tender.

5. With slotted spoon, remove chicken from slow cooker. Remove chicken from bones; discard bones. Cut chicken into pieces; return chicken to stew. If desired, add salt and pepper to taste.

NUTRITION INFORMATION PER SERVING: Serving Size: ⅙ of Recipe • Calories 265 • Calories from Fat 65 • % Daily Value: Total Fat 7g 11% • Saturated Fat 2g 10% • Cholesterol 45mg 15% • Sodium 980mg 41% • Total Carbohydrate 35g 12% • Dietary Fiber 6g 24% • Sugars 8g • Protein 22g • Vitamin A 16% • Vitamin C 18% • Calcium 4% • Iron 18% • **DIETARY EXCHANGES:** 2 Starch, 1 Vegetable, 2 Very Lean Meat **OR** 2 Carbohydrate, 1 Vegetable, 2 Very Lean Meat

KIDS CAN HELP

Not only will kids enjoy eating this stew, they can have fun making it, too. Your young helper can lend a hand by shaking the bag of chicken, vegetables and coating ingredients.

winter vegetable stew

YIELD: 8 SERVINGS

Prep Time: 20 minutes (Ready in 10 hours 40 minutes)

1 (28-oz.) can Italian-style plum tomatoes

4 medium red potatoes, cut into ¹/₂-inch pieces

4 medium stalks celery, cut into ¹/₂-inch pieces (2 cups)

3 medium carrots, cut into ¹/₂-inch pieces (1¹/₂ cups)

2 medium parsnips, peeled, cut into ¹/₂-inch pieces

2 medium leeks, cut into ¹/₂-inch pieces

1 (14-oz.) can vegetable or chicken broth

¹/₂ teaspoon salt

¹/₂ teaspoon dried thyme leaves

¹/₂ teaspoon dried rosemary leaves

3 tablespoons cold water

3 tablespoons cornstarch

1. Drain tomatoes, reserving liquid. Cut up tomatoes. In 4- to 5-quart slow cooker, combine tomatoes, reserved tomato liquid and all remaining ingredients except water and cornstarch.

2. Cover; cook on low setting for 8 to 10 hours.

3. In small bowl, blend water and cornstarch until smooth. Gradually stir into stew. Increase heat setting to high; cover and cook an additional 20 minutes or until thickened, stirring occasionally.

NUTRITION INFORMATION PER SERVING: Serving Size: ⅛ of Recipe • Calories 120 • Calories from Fat 0 • % Daily Value: Total Fat 0g 0% • Saturated Fat 0g 0% • Cholesterol 0mg 0% • Sodium 550mg 23% • Total Carbohydrate 31g 10% • Dietary Fiber 5g 20% • Sugars 7g • Protein 4g • Vitamin A 94% • Vitamin C 26% • Calcium 8% • Iron 10% • **DIETARY EXCHANGES:** ½ Starch, 4 Vegetable **OR** 1 Carbohydrate, 4 Vegetable

DOUGHBOY TIP

Parsnips are root vegetables that look like creamy white carrots and have a slightly sweet flavor. If you don't have any on hand, feel free to use carrots instead.

vegetable, lentil and pasta stew

YIELD: 4 SERVINGS

Prep Time: 10 minutes (Ready in 12 hours 40 minutes)

¾ cup dried lentils, sorted, rinsed

1 cup sliced celery

½ cup coarsely chopped green bell pepper

3½ cups vegetable broth

1 (11.5-oz.) can vegetable juice cocktail

2 oz. (⅓ cup) uncooked orzo or rosamarina (rice-shaped pasta)

1 teaspoon dried thyme leaves

1. In 3½- to 4-quart slow cooker, combine lentils, celery, bell pepper and broth; mix well.

2. Cover; cook on low setting for 10 to 12 hours.

3. About 30 minutes before serving, stir vegetable juice cocktail, orzo and thyme into stew. Increase heat setting to high; cover and cook an additional 25 to 30 minutes or until orzo is tender.

NUTRITION INFORMATION PER SERVING: Serving Size: ¼ of Recipe • Calories 230 • Calories from Fat 20 • % Daily Value: Total Fat 2g 3% • Saturated Fat 0g 0% • Cholesterol 0mg 0% • Sodium 1470mg 61% • Total Carbohydrate 40g 13% • Dietary Fiber 13g 52% • Sugars 8g • Protein 13g • Vitamin A 25% • Vitamin C 50% • Calcium 4% • Iron 25% • **DIETARY EXCHANGES:** 2 Starch, 1½ Vegetable, ½ Very Lean Meat **OR** 2 Carbohydrate, 1½ Vegetable, ½ Very Lean Meat

DOUGHBOY TIP

Lentils come in many colors—brown, red and yellow. You can find brown lentils in most supermarkets, but you may have to look in a co-op or Middle Eastern or East Indian market to find the red and yellow varieties.

ratatouille bean stew

1 cup dried garbanzo beans or chickpeas, sorted, rinsed

½ cup chopped onion

2 garlic cloves, minced

1 (14-oz.) can chicken broth

1 (4.5-oz.) jar sliced mushrooms, drained

¼ teaspoon salt

1 large zucchini, sliced

1 medium red or green bell pepper, cut into pieces

1 teaspoon dried Italian seasoning

1 (14.5-oz.) can diced tomatoes with Italian-style herbs, undrained

1. Soak garbanzo beans in enough water to cover for at least 8 hours.

2. Drain beans, discarding water. In 3½- to 4-quart slow cooker, combine beans, onion, garlic, broth, mushrooms and salt; mix well.

3. Cover; cook on low setting for 10 to 12 hours.

4. About 35 minutes before serving, stir zucchini, bell pepper, Italian seasoning and tomatoes into stew. Increase heat setting to high; cover and cook an additional 30 to 35 minutes or until vegetables are tender.

NUTRITION INFORMATION PER SERVING: Serving Size: ⅕ of Recipe • Calories 220 • Calories from Fat 25 • % Daily Value: Total Fat 3g 5% • Saturated Fat 0g 0% • Cholesterol 0mg 0% • Sodium 640mg 27% • Total Carbohydrate 37g 12% • Dietary Fiber 10g 40% • Sugars 9g • Protein 12g • Vitamin A 30% • Vitamin C 50% • Calcium 10% • Iron 20% • **DIETARY EXCHANGES:** 1½ Starch, ½ Fruit, 1 Vegetable, 1 Very Lean Meat, ½ Fat **OR** 2 Carbohydrate, 1 Vegetable, 1 Very Lean Meat, ½ Fat

DOUGHBOY TIP

It's easy to make this recipe vegetarian. Simply use vegetable broth in place of the chicken broth.

texas chili

YIELD: 6 SERVINGS

Prep Time: 15 minutes (Ready in 10 hours 15 minutes)

1½ lb. beef top round steak, trimmed of fat, cut into ¾-inch cubes

1 small onion, finely chopped

2 garlic cloves, minced

1 (28-oz.) can diced tomatoes, undrained

1 (8-oz.) can tomato sauce

1 (15- or 15.5-oz.) can pinto beans, undrained

1 (4.5-oz.) can chopped green chiles

3 teaspoons chili powder

1 teaspoon cumin

1. In 4- to 6-quart slow cooker, combine all ingredients; mix well.

2. Cover; cook on low setting for 8 to 10 hours.

NUTRITION INFORMATION PER SERVING: Serving Size: ⅙ of Recipe • Calories 250 • Calories from Fat 35 • % Daily Value: Total Fat 4g 6% • Saturated Fat 1g 5% • Cholesterol 60mg 20% • Sodium 710mg 30% • Total Carbohydrate 31g 10% • Dietary Fiber 9g 36% • Sugars 7g • Protein 31g • Vitamin A 26% • Vitamin C 26% • Calcium 10% • Iron 30% • **DIETARY EXCHANGES:** 2 Starch, 3 Very Lean Meat **OR** 2 Carbohydrate, 3 Very Lean Meat

SERVE WITH

Chunks of meat and spicy seasonings give this chili a Texas touch. You'll want to have bowls of your favorite chili toppers such as sour cream, shredded Cheddar cheese and sliced green onions ready and waiting for the first steaming serving. Don't forget to bake up some refrigerated cornbread twists, which are perfect for chili dipping and dunking.

chunky beef and pork chili

YIELD: 6 SERVINGS

Prep Time: 20 minutes (Ready in 10 hours 50 minutes)

1 lb. beef round steak, trimmed of fat, cut into ¾-inch pieces

1 lb. pork shoulder steak, trimmed of fat, cut into ¾-inch pieces

1 cup chopped onions

2 garlic cloves, minced

1 (15-oz.) can tomato sauce

1 (12-oz.) jar chunky-style salsa

2 teaspoons dried Mexican seasoning

1 medium green bell pepper, chopped (1 cup)

1. In 3½- to 6-quart slow cooker, combine all ingredients except bell pepper; mix well.

2. Cover; cook on low setting for 8 to 10 hours.

3. About 30 minutes before serving, stir bell pepper into chili. Cover; cook on low setting an additional 15 to 30 minutes or until bell pepper is tender.

NUTRITION INFORMATION PER SERVING: Serving Size: ⅙ of Recipe • Calories 265 • Calories from Fat 100 • % Daily Value: Total Fat 11g 17% • Saturated Fat 4g 20% • Cholesterol 85mg 28% • Sodium 740mg 31% • Total Carbohydrate 13g 4% • Dietary Fiber 3g 12% • Sugars 6g • Protein 32g • Vitamin A 26% • Vitamin C 30% • Calcium 4% • Iron 18% • **DIETARY EXCHANGES:** 2 Vegetable, 4 Lean Meat **OR** 1 Carbohydrate, 2 Vegetable, 4 Lean Meat

MAKE IT SPECIAL

There's nothing like a bowl of hot chili to warm you from the inside out. For a cool zing, mix a tablespoon or two of fresh lime juice into 1 cup of sour cream. Spoon on top of the chili, and garnish with chopped fresh cilantro or sliced green onions. For a double dose of lime, sprinkle with crushed lime-flavored tortilla chips.

meaty two-bean chili

YIELD: 6 SERVINGS
Prep Time: 20 minutes (Ready in 8 hours 20 minutes)

1 lb. lean ground beef

½ lb. bulk Italian pork sausage

½ cup chopped onion

1 (28-oz.) can whole tomatoes, undrained, cut up

1 (15-oz.) can tomato sauce

1 teaspoon sugar

1 to 2 teaspoons chili powder

1 to 1½ teaspoons cumin

1 teaspoon dried oregano leaves

1 (15-oz.) can spicy chili beans, undrained

1 (15-oz.) can garbanzo beans or chickpeas, drained, rinsed

1. In large skillet, cook ground beef, sausage and onion until ground beef and sausage are thoroughly cooked, stirring frequently. Drain.

2. In 4- to 6-quart slow cooker, combine ground beef mixture and all remaining ingredients; mix well.

3. Cover; cook on low setting for 7 to 8 hours.

NUTRITION INFORMATION PER SERVING: Serving Size: ⅙ of Recipe • Calories 440 • Calories from Fat 180 • % Daily Value: Total Fat 20g 31% • Saturated Fat 7g 35% • Cholesterol 65mg 22% • Sodium 1570mg 65% • Total Carbohydrate 44g 15% • Dietary Fiber 11g 44% • Sugars 10g • Protein 32g • Vitamin A 30% • Vitamin C 32% • Calcium 12% • Iron 36% • **DIETARY EXCHANGES:** 3 Starch, 3 Medium-Fat Meat **OR** 3 Carbohydrate, 3 Medium-Fat Meat

MAKE IT SPECIAL
Go for the green when topping this hearty beef and bean combination! Sprinkle individual bowls of chili with diced avocado, or dollop each serving with a spoonful of guacamole. Finish each bowl with chopped fresh cilantro and chopped jalapeño chiles.

spicy vegetarian chili

YIELD: 6 SERVINGS

Prep Time: 10 minutes (Ready in 6 hours 10 minutes)

1 (15.5-oz.) can spicy chili beans, undrained

1 (15- or 15.5-oz.) can pinto beans, undrained

1 (15- or 15.5-oz.) can dark red kidney beans, drained

1 (14.5-oz.) can chili-style chunky tomatoes, undrained

1 cup chopped onions

2 to 3 teaspoons chili powder

⅛ teaspoon ground red pepper (cayenne)

1. In 3½- to 6-quart slow cooker, combine all ingredients; mix well.

2. Cover; cook on low setting for 5 to 6 hours. Stir well before serving.

NUTRITION INFORMATION PER SERVING: Serving Size: ⅙ of Recipe • Calories 210 • Calories from Fat 10 • % Daily Value: Total Fat 1g 2% • Saturated Fat 0g 0% • Cholesterol 0mg 0% • Sodium 620mg 26% • Total Carbohydrate 49g 16% • Dietary Fiber 12g 48% • Sugars 6g • Protein 15g • Vitamin A 18% • Vitamin C 20% • Calcium 10% • Iron 30% • **DIETARY EXCHANGES:** 2 Starch, 3 Vegetable **OR** 3 Carbohydrate, 3 Vegetable

DOUGHBOY TIP

Use any canned beans that you have on hand for the pinto or kidney beans. You may want to try great northern, black, garbanzo or lima beans.

slow-cooked sandwiches

Hot Beef Sandwiches au Jus 132

Easy Barbecued Beef Sandwiches 133

Double-Onion Beef Sandwiches 134

Philly Cheese Steak Sandwiches 135

Southwest Beef Sandwiches 136

So-Easy Sloppy Joes 137

Creamy Beef Pitas 138

Cheeseburger Sandwiches 139

Gingered Pork Wraps 140

Bratwurst and Sauerkraut 141

Pulled-Pork Burritos 142

Open-Faced Pizza Sandwiches 143

Sweet-and-Saucy Ham Sandwiches 144

Jerked Chicken Hoagies 145

Greek Chicken Pita Folds 147

Hot Turkey Sandwiches 148

Tex-Mex Wraps with Turkey 149

Georgia-Style Barbecued Turkey Sandwiches 150

Italian Ground Turkey Rolls 152

BBQ Veggie Joes 153

ITALIAN GROUND TURKEY ROLLS, PAGE 152

hot beef sandwiches au jus

YIELD: 16 SANDWICHES
Prep Time: 15 minutes (Ready in 10 hours 15 minutes)

1 (4- to 5-lb.) beef rump roast

1 (1-oz.) pkg. dry onion soup mix

2 teaspoons sugar

1 teaspoon dried oregano leaves

2 (10½-oz.) cans condensed beef broth

1 (12-oz.) can beer or nonalcoholic beer

2 garlic cloves, minced

16 onion buns, split

1. Place beef roast in 3½- to 4-quart slow cooker. In medium bowl, combine all remaining ingredients except buns; mix well. Pour over beef.

2. Cover; cook on low setting for 8 to 10 hours.

3. Remove beef from slow cooker; place on cutting board or large plate. Slice beef with knife or shred with 2 forks; place in buns. If desired, skim fat from juices in slow cooker. Serve sandwiches with individual portions of juices for dipping.

NUTRITION INFORMATION PER SERVING: Serving Size: 1 Sandwich • Calories 310 • Calories from Fat 110 • % Daily Value: Total Fat 12g 18% • Saturated Fat 4g 20% • Cholesterol 75mg 25% • Sodium 640mg 27% • Total Carbohydrate 21g 7% • Dietary Fiber 1g 4% • Sugars 2g • Protein 28g • Vitamin A 0% • Vitamin C 0% • Calcium 4% • Iron 20% • DIETARY EXCHANGES: 1½ Starch, 3½ Lean Meat OR 1½ Carbohydrate, 3½ Lean Meat

SERVE WITH

Planning a casual get-together with friends or family? Instead of French rolls, use small buns and let guests build their own sandwiches. Spoon a small amount of broth from the slow cooker into small bowls for dipping. Set out a basket of chips and a tray of raw veggies and dip. Brownies are a can't-miss choice for dessert.

easy barbecued beef sandwiches

YIELD: 24 SANDWICHES

Prep Time: 15 minutes (Ready in 6 hours 35 minutes)

4 lb. boneless beef round steak (¾ inch thick), trimmed of fat, cut into pieces

2 cups ketchup

1 cup cola-flavored carbonated beverage

1 tablespoon prepared horseradish

½ cup chopped onion

2 garlic cloves, minced

24 sandwich buns, split

1. Arrange beef in 3½- to 4-quart slow cooker. Add all remaining ingredients except buns; mix well.

2. Cover; cook on high setting for 5 to 6 hours.

3. About 30 minutes before serving, remove beef from slow cooker; place on large plate. Shred beef with 2 forks; return to slow cooker and mix well. Cover; cook on high setting an additional 20 minutes or until beef is moistened and thoroughly heated.

4. With slotted spoon, spoon about ⅓ cup beef mixture into each bun. Mixture can be kept warm for several hours on low setting.

NUTRITION INFORMATION PER SERVING: Serving Size: 1 Sandwich • Calories 230 • Calories from Fat 45 • % Daily Value: Total Fat 5g 8% • Saturated Fat 1g 5% • Cholesterol 40mg 13% • Sodium 510mg 21% • Total Carbohydrate 29g 10% • Dietary Fiber 2g 8% • Sugars 11g • Protein 19g • Vitamin A 6% • Vitamin C 2% • Calcium 6% • Iron 16% • **DIETARY EXCHANGES:** 1½ Starch, ½ Fruit, 2½ Very Lean Meat **OR** 2 Carbohydrate, 2½ Very Lean Meat

DOUGHBOY TIP

Barbecued beef is great to have on hand when you need a super-simple sandwich idea. Place the cooked beef in pint-size freezer containers, and freeze up to 4 months. To thaw frozen barbecued beef, place in the refrigerator for about 8 hours. When you're ready to serve it, just reheat the beef in a saucepan on top of the stove or in the microwave. You can then put it in a preheated slow cooker to keep it warm.

double-onion beef sandwiches

YIELD: 8 SANDWICHES

Prep Time: 15 minutes (Ready in 10 hours 15 minutes)

3 large garlic cloves, minced

1 tablespoon Worcestershire sauce

½ teaspoon coarsely ground black pepper

1 (3-lb.) fresh beef brisket (not corned beef)

1 medium onion, thinly sliced

1 (1.3-oz.) pkg. dry onion soup mix

½ cup water

8 individual French breads or crusty rolls

1. In small bowl, combine garlic, Worcestershire sauce and pepper; mix well. Rub on both sides of beef brisket. Cut beef in half or thirds to fit slow cooker. Place sliced onion in 3½- to 6-quart slow cooker. Top with beef pieces. Sprinkle with soup mix. Add water.

2. Cover; cook on low setting for 8 to 10 hours.

3. Remove beef from slow cooker; place on cutting board. Cut beef across grain into thin slices. Skim fat from juices in slow cooker. Return beef to slow cooker; mix well. Cut breads horizontally in half. Spoon beef mixture onto bottom halves of buns. Drizzle with juices. Cover with top halves of buns.

NUTRITION INFORMATION PER SERVING: Serving Size: 1 Sandwich • Calories 390 • Calories from Fat 125 • % Daily Value: Total Fat 14g 22% • Saturated Fat 5g 25% • Cholesterol 95mg 32% • Sodium 780mg 33% • Total Carbohydrate 27g 9% • Dietary Fiber 2g 8% • Sugars 3g • Protein 41g • Vitamin A 2% • Vitamin C 2% • Calcium 6% • Iron 26% • **DIETARY EXCHANGES:** 2 Starch, 4 Lean Meat **OR** 2 Carbohydrate, 4 Lean Meat

DOUGHBOY TIP

Save yourself the time of chopping by picking up a jar of chopped garlic. When a recipe calls for a clove of garlic, you'll need ½ teaspoon chopped garlic.

philly cheese steak sandwiches

YIELD: 4 SANDWICHES

Prep Time: 25 minutes (Ready in 8 hours 25 minutes)

1 tablespoon margarine or butter, melted

2 medium onions, sliced

1 lb. boneless beef round steak (1 inch thick), trimmed of fat, cut into 1 x ¼-inch strips

2 teaspoons garlic-pepper blend

½ teaspoon salt

1 large green bell pepper, cut into rings

¼ cup water

1 teaspoon beef-flavor instant bouillon

4 hoagie buns, split

4 (1-oz.) slices provolone cheese, halved

1. In medium bowl, combine margarine and onions; mix to coat. Sprinkle beef with garlic-pepper blend and salt.

2. In 3- to 4-quart slow cooker, layer half of the onions, all of the beef and the bell pepper. Top with remaining half of onions. In measuring cup, combine water and bouillon; stir until dissolved. Pour over mixture in slow cooker.

3. Cover; cook on low setting for 6 to 8 hours.

4. About 10 minutes before serving, place bun halves, cut side up, on ungreased cookie sheet. With slotted spoon, place beef mixture on bottom halves of buns. Top each with 2 pieces of cheese. Broil 2 to 3 inches from heat until cheese is melted and top halves of buns are toasted. Place top halves over cheese.

NUTRITION INFORMATION PER SERVING: Serving Size: 1 Sandwich • Calories 425 • Calories from Fat 155 • % Daily Value: Total Fat 17g 26% • Saturated Fat 7g 35% • Cholesterol 85mg 28% • Sodium 1240mg 52% • Total Carbohydrate 35g 12% • Dietary Fiber 3g 12% • Sugars 5g • Protein 36g • Vitamin A 12% • Vitamin C 32% • Calcium 28% • Iron 22% • **DIETARY EXCHANGES:** 2 Starch, 1 Vegetable, 4 Lean Meat, ½ Fat **OR** 2 Carbohydrate, 1 Vegetable, 4 Lean Meat, ½ Fat

DOUGHBOY TIP

These cheesy beef sandwiches are full of possibilities. Mozzarella cheese can be used instead of the provolone. If you don't have hoagie buns, use crusty French or kaiser rolls instead.

southwest beef sandwiches

YIELD: 8 SANDWICHES
Prep Time: 15 minutes (Ready in 8 hours 15 minutes)

1½ cups chopped onions

1½ cups chunky-style salsa

3 tablespoons chopped fresh cilantro

3 garlic cloves, minced

2 teaspoons cumin

2 teaspoons chili powder

¼ teaspoon salt

1½ lb. beef flank steak, cut into 6 pieces

8 sandwich buns, split

1. In 3½- to 4-quart slow cooker, combine all ingredients except beef and buns. Add beef; mix well.

2. Cover; cook on low setting for at least 8 hours or on high setting for 4 hours.

3. Remove beef from slow cooker; place on large plate. Shred beef with 2 forks; return to slow cooker and mix well. Spoon ⅓ to ½ cup beef mixture into each bun.

NUTRITION INFORMATION PER SERVING: Serving Size: 1 Sandwich • Calories 250 • Calories from Fat 70 • % Daily Value: Total Fat 8g 12% • Saturated Fat 3g 15% • Cholesterol 35mg 12% • Sodium 560mg 23% • Total Carbohydrate 28g 9% • Dietary Fiber 2g 8% • Sugars 8g • Protein 17g • Vitamin A 8% • Vitamin C 10% • Calcium 8% • Iron 20% • **DIETARY EXCHANGES:** 2 Starch, 1½ Lean Meat **OR** 2 Carbohydrate, 1½ Lean Meat

MAKE IT SPECIAL

Sometimes a good sandwich is all it takes to satisfy. A sprinkle of shredded Cheddar cheese and a dollop of sour cream turn these bold and spicy sandwiches into a sensation.

so-easy sloppy joes

YIELD: 16 SANDWICHES

Prep Time: 20 minutes (Ready in 5 hours 20 minutes)

3 lb. lean ground beef

1 cup chopped onions

1 cup chopped celery

½ cup chopped green bell pepper

1 (12-oz.) bottle chili sauce

1 (6-oz.) can tomato paste

2 to 3 tablespoons brown sugar

2 tablespoons Worcestershire sauce

¼ teaspoon pepper

16 sandwich buns, split

1. In large skillet, cook ground beef, onions, celery and bell pepper until beef is thoroughly cooked, stirring frequently. Drain.

2. In 3½- to 4-quart slow cooker, combine ground beef mixture and all remaining ingredients except buns; mix well.

3. Cover; cook on low setting for 3 to 5 hours, stirring occasionally. Spoon beef mixture into buns.

NUTRITION INFORMATION PER SERVING: Serving Size: 1 Sandwich • Calories 335 • Calories from Fat 125 • % Daily Value: Total Fat 14g 22% • Saturated Fat 5g 25% • Cholesterol 50mg 17% • Sodium 690mg 29% • Total Carbohydrate 34g 11% • Dietary Fiber 2g 8% • Sugars 14g • Protein 20g • Vitamin A 12% • Vitamin C 6% • Calcium 8% • Iron 18% • **DIETARY EXCHANGES:** 2 Starch, 1 Vegetable, 2 Medium-Fat Meat **OR** 2 Carbohydrate, 1 Vegetable, 2 Medium-Fat Meat

MAKE IT SPECIAL

Serve **Sloppy Joe Shortcakes**—guaranteed to be a crowd pleaser! Bake a 12-oz. can refrigerated buttermilk flaky biscuits as directed on can. Split biscuits into halves. Spoon meat mixture on bottom halves of biscuits; add the biscuit tops. Spoon additional meat mixture on top, and sprinkle with shredded Cheddar cheese.

creamy beef pitas

YIELD: 16 SANDWICHES; 8 SERVINGS

Prep Time: 25 minutes (Ready in 9 hours 25 minutes)

2½ lb. boneless beef top round steak, trimmed of fat, cut into 2-inch pieces

3 (4.5-oz.) jars sliced mushrooms, drained

1 medium onion, halved, sliced

1 tablespoon beef-flavor instant bouillon

¾ teaspoon pepper

⅛ teaspoon nutmeg

½ cup sour cream

¼ cup all-purpose flour

8 pita (pocket) breads, cut in half, heated

1. In 3½- to 4-quart slow cooker, combine beef, mushrooms, onion, bouillon, pepper and nutmeg; mix well.

2. Cover; cook on low setting for 7 to 9 hours.

3. About 15 minutes before serving, in small bowl, blend sour cream and flour until smooth. Add ⅓ cup hot liquid from slow cooker; mix well. Stir flour mixture into beef mixture. Cover; cook on low setting an additional 10 minutes or until thickened.

4. Carefully open warm pita bread halves. Spoon about ¾ cup beef mixture into each pita half.

NUTRITION INFORMATION PER SERVING: Serving Size: ⅛ of Recipe • Calories 400 • Calories from Fat 80 • % Daily Value: Total Fat 9g 14% • Saturated Fat 4g 20% • Cholesterol 80mg 27% • Sodium 850mg 35% • Total Carbohydrate 41g 14% • Dietary Fiber 3g 12% • Sugars 3g • Protein 38g • Vitamin A 2% • Vitamin C 0% • Calcium 8% • Iron 25% • **DIETARY EXCHANGES:** 2½ Starch, 4½ Very Lean Meat, 1 Fat **OR** 2½ Carbohydrate, 4½ Very Lean Meat, 1 Fat

SERVE WITH

Try serving this beef mixture over baked potatoes rather than using it as a sandwich filling. Or spoon it over hot cooked noodles or rice.

cheeseburger sandwiches

YIELD: 8 SANDWICHES

Prep Time: 20 minutes (Ready in 7 hours 20 minutes)

1½ lb. lean ground beef

½ teaspoon garlic-pepper blend

1 (8-oz.) pkg. pasteurized process cheese spread, diced (2 cups)

2 tablespoons milk

1 medium green bell pepper, chopped (1 cup)

¼ cup chopped onion

2 garlic cloves, minced

8 sandwich buns, split

1. In large skillet, cook ground beef and garlic-pepper blend until beef is thoroughly cooked, stirring frequently. Drain.

2. In 3½- to 4-quart slow cooker, combine cooked ground beef and all remaining ingredients except buns; mix well.

3. Cover; cook on low setting for 6 to 7 hours. Spoon beef mixture into buns.

NUTRITION INFORMATION PER SERVING: Serving Size: 1 Sandwich • Calories 370 • Calories from Fat 170 • % Daily Value: Total Fat 19g 29% • Saturated Fat 9g 45% • Cholesterol 70mg 23% • Sodium 690mg 29% • Total Carbohydrate 26g 9% • Dietary Fiber 1g 4% • Sugars 8g • Protein 24g • Vitamin A 6% • Vitamin C 10% • Calcium 25% • Iron 15% • **DIETARY EXCHANGES:** 1½ Starch, 3 Medium-Fat Meat, ½ Fat **OR** 1½ Carbohydrate, 3 Medium-Fat Meat, ½ Fat

SERVE WITH

Tonight, why not make a date with the kids? They'll love this made-from-scratch spin on one of their favorite foods. Add a side of french fries, dill pickles and of course ketchup and mustard. Chocolate milk shakes are a happy ending to this far-from-fast-food meal.

gingered pork wraps

YIELD: 12 SANDWICHES

Prep Time: 20 minutes (Ready in 10 hours 20 minutes)

1 (3½-lb.) boneless rolled pork loin roast

2 tablespoons grated gingerroot

2 tablespoons dry sherry, if desired

1 garlic clove, minced

½ cup hoisin sauce

6 dried shiitake mushrooms

12 (10- to 12-inch) flour tortillas

2 teaspoons sesame oil

4 cups shredded Chinese (napa) cabbage

1 bunch green onions, cut into 2 x 1/16-inch slivers (about ¾ cup)

1. Place pork roast in 4- to 6-quart slow cooker. In small bowl, combine gingerroot, sherry, garlic and 3 tablespoons of the hoisin sauce; mix well. Spoon mixture over roast. Snap off and discard stems from dried mushrooms; crumble mushrooms over roast.

2. Cover; cook on low setting for 8 to 10 hours.

3. About 15 minutes before serving, heat oven to 300°F. Brush tortillas with sesame oil; stack on sheet of foil. Wrap tightly. Heat packet at 300°F. for 10 minutes.

4. Meanwhile, remove pork from slow cooker; place on large plate. Stir cabbage into juices in slow cooker. Increase heat setting to high; cover and cook an additional 5 minutes or until cabbage is wilted.

5. Shred pork with 2 forks; return to slow cooker. Spread each warm tortilla with 1 teaspoon remaining hoisin sauce. Top each with about ¾ cup pork mixture and 1 tablespoon onions; roll up.

NUTRITION INFORMATION PER SERVING: Serving Size: 1 Sandwich • Calories 500 • Calories from Fat 140 • % Daily Value: Total Fat 16g 25% • Saturated Fat 5g 25% • Cholesterol 80mg 27% • Sodium 660mg 28% • Total Carbohydrate 53g 18% • Dietary Fiber 3g 12% • Sugars 7g • Protein 36g • Vitamin A 15% • Vitamin C 15% • Calcium 15% • Iron 25% • **DIETARY EXCHANGES:** 3½ Starch, 3½ Lean Meat, ½ Fat OR 3½ Carbohydrate, 3½ Lean Meat, ½ Fat

DOUGHBOY TIP
Sesame oil has a nice nutty flavor that tastes great in this recipe, but vegetable oil can be used instead. To add an extra hint of sesame flavor, sprinkle the filling with toasted sesame seed before wrapping it up.

bratwurst and sauerkraut

YIELD: 6 SANDWICHES

Prep Time: 5 minutes (Ready in 5 hours 5 minutes)

4 cooked bratwurst (about 4 oz. each), cut into ½-inch slices

2 (14-oz.) cans sauerkraut, drained

⅓ cup firmly packed brown sugar

6 hot dog or bratwurst buns, split

1. In 3½- to 6-quart slow cooker, combine all ingredients except buns; mix well.

2. Cover; cook on low setting for 4 to 5 hours. Spoon bratwurst mixture into buns.

NUTRITION INFORMATION PER SERVING: Serving Size: 1 Sandwich • Calories 410 • Calories from Fat 205 • % Daily Value: Total Fat 23g 35% • Saturated Fat 8g 40% • Cholesterol 45mg 15% • Sodium 1910mg 80% • Total Carbohydrate 41g 14% • Dietary Fiber 5g 20% • Sugars 18g • Protein 14g • Vitamin A 0% • Vitamin C 16% • Calcium 12% • Iron 24% • **DIETARY EXCHANGES:** 2 Starch, 2 Vegetable, ½ High-Fat Meat, 3½ Fat **OR** 2 Carbohydrate, 2 Vegetable, ½ High-Fat Meat, 3½ Fat

DOUGHBOY TIP

Be sure to check that the bratwursts you buy are fully cooked rather than fresh. The juice that would be released from fresh bratwursts during cooking would add too much liquid to the mixture.

pulled-pork burritos

YIELD: 9 SANDWICHES

Prep Time: 10 minutes (Ready in 10 hours 10 minutes)

1 (2- to 2½-lb.) boneless pork loin roast

1 medium onion, thinly sliced

2 cups barbecue sauce

¾ cup chunky-style salsa

3 tablespoons chili powder

3 teaspoons dried Mexican seasoning

9 (8- to 10-inch) flour tortillas

1. Place pork roast in 3½- to 6-quart slow cooker. Arrange onion on top. In small bowl, combine all remaining ingredients except tortillas; mix well. Pour over pork.

2. Cover; cook on low setting for 8 to 10 hours.

3. Remove pork from slow cooker; place on large plate. With 2 forks, pull pork into shreds. Pour sauce from slow cooker into bowl; stir in pork. Spoon pork mixture onto each tortilla; roll up.

NUTRITION INFORMATION PER SERVING: Serving Size: 1 Sandwich • Calories 435 • Calories from Fat 125 • % Daily Value: Total Fat 14g 22% • Saturated Fat 4g 20% • Cholesterol 80mg 27% • Sodium 930mg 39% • Total Carbohydrate 47g 16% • Dietary Fiber 3g 12% • Sugars 17g • Protein 33g • Vitamin A 24% • Vitamin C 6% • Calcium 10% • Iron 20% • **DIETARY EXCHANGES:** 2 Starch, 1 Fruit, 4 Lean Meat **OR** 3 Carbohydrate, 4 Lean Meat

DOUGHBOY TIP
The beauty of slow-cooked pork is that it becomes so tender you can shred, or "pull," it with a fork. If you're lucky enough to have leftovers, wrap up the burritos in foil and freeze them up to 2 months. To reheat, transfer the wrapped burritos to a 350°F. oven for 20 to 25 minutes. Leftover shredded pork can also be stored in the refrigerator for up to 4 days or frozen up to 4 months.

open-faced pizza sandwiches

YIELD: 6 SANDWICHES

Prep Time: 25 minutes (Ready in 8 hours 25 minutes)

1½ lb. bulk Italian pork sausage

½ cup chopped onion

1 medium green bell pepper, chopped (1 cup)

1 (4.5-oz.) jar sliced mushrooms, drained

1 (6-oz.) can tomato paste

1 (15-oz.) can pizza sauce

1 (9.5-oz.) pkg. frozen herb or cheese Texas toast

3 oz. (¾ cup) finely shredded mozzarella cheese

1. In large skillet, cook sausage and onion over medium heat until sausage is no longer pink, stirring occasionally. Drain.

2. In 3½- to 4-quart slow cooker, combine cooked sausage and onion, bell pepper, mushrooms and tomato paste; mix well. Top with pizza sauce.

3. Cover; cook on low setting for 6 to 8 hours.

4. About 10 minutes before serving, heat toast as directed on package. Stir sausage mixture. Spoon about ¾ cup sausage mixture onto each warm toast slice. Sprinkle each with 2 tablespoons cheese.

NUTRITION INFORMATION PER SERVING: Serving Size: 1 Sandwich • Calories 550 • Calories from Fat 290 • % Daily Value: Total Fat 32g 49% • Saturated Fat 11g 55% • Cholesterol 75mg 25% • Sodium 1510mg 63% • Total Carbohydrate 37g 12% • Dietary Fiber 4g 16% • Sugars 5g • Protein 29g • Vitamin A 25% • Vitamin C 40% • Calcium 25% • Iron 20% • **DIETARY EXCHANGES:** 2½ Starch, 3 High-Fat Meat, 1 Fat **OR** 2½ Carbohydrate, 3 High-Fat Meat, 1 Fat

DOUGHBOY TIP

Texas toast is thick slices of French bread that are coated with garlic butter. You'll usually find it in the freezer case of your supermarket. If it's not available, you can use sliced French bread spread with garlic butter.

sweet-and-saucy ham sandwiches

YIELD: 12 SANDWICHES
Prep Time: 10 minutes (Ready in 4 hours 25 minutes)

1½ lb. cooked smoked ham, ground (4 cups)

1 cup firmly packed brown sugar

½ cup Dijon mustard

¼ cup chopped green bell pepper

1 tablespoon instant minced onion

1 (20-oz.) can crushed pineapple in unsweetened juice, undrained

12 sandwich buns, split

1. In 3½- to 6-quart slow cooker, combine all ingredients except buns; mix well.

2. Cover; cook on low setting for 3 to 4 hours.

3. About 15 minutes before serving, uncover slow cooker. Increase heat setting to high; cook, uncovered, an additional 10 to 15 minutes or until desired consistency. Stir well before serving. Spoon ham mixture into buns.

NUTRITION INFORMATION PER SERVING: Serving Size: 1 Sandwich • Calories 330 • Calories from Fat 70 • % Daily Value: Total Fat 8g 12% • Saturated Fat 2g 10% • Cholesterol 35mg 12% • Sodium 1350mg 56% • Total Carbohydrate 49g 16% • Dietary Fiber 2g 8% • Sugars 31g • Protein 17g • Vitamin A 0% • Vitamin C 6% • Calcium 8% • Iron 14% • **DIETARY EXCHANGES:** 1 Starch, 2 Fruit, 1 Vegetable, 2 Lean Meat **OR** 3 Carbohydrate, 1 Vegetable, 2 Lean Meat

DOUGHBOY TIP
If you have a food processor, use it to finely chop the ham instead of grinding it. Or better yet, ask your butcher to grind it for you.

jerked chicken hoagies

YIELD: 4 SANDWICHES

Prep Time: 15 minutes (Ready in 8 hours 15 minutes)

3 tablespoons dried Caribbean jerk seasoning

3 lb. boneless skinless chicken thighs

1 large red or green bell pepper, chopped (1½ cups)

1 cup chopped onions

½ cup chicken broth

¼ cup ketchup

4 hoagie buns, split

1. Rub jerk seasoning generously over chicken thighs. In 3½- to 4-quart slow cooker, combine bell pepper and onions. Place chicken over vegetables.

2. In small bowl, combine broth and ketchup; mix well. Pour broth mixture over chicken.

3. Cover; cook on low setting for 6 to 8 hours.

4. Remove chicken from slow cooker; place on large plate. Shred chicken with 2 forks; return to slow cooker and mix well. With slotted spoon, spoon chicken mixture into buns.

NUTRITION INFORMATION PER SERVING: Serving Size: 1 Sandwich • Calories 780 • Calories from Fat 260 • % Daily Value: Total Fat 29g 45% • Saturated Fat 8g 40% • Cholesterol 215mg 72% • Sodium 1720mg 72% • Total Carbohydrate 60g 20% • Dietary Fiber 5g 20% • Sugars 6g • Protein 69g • Vitamin A 10% • Vitamin C 35% • Calcium 15% • Iron 35% • **DIETARY EXCHANGES:** 4 Starch, 8 Lean Meat, ½ Fat **OR** 4 Carbohydrate, 8 Lean Meat, ½ Fat

SERVE WITH

Treat your family to a colorful Caribbean meal. Serve these flavorful sandwiches with an exotic fruit salad of diced pineapple, papaya, mango, kiwi fruit and banana. Add a basket of purchased sweet potato chips and a pitcher of tropical fruit punch.

greek chicken pita folds

YIELD: 4 SANDWICHES

Prep Time: 15 minutes (Ready in 8 hours 15 minutes)

1 medium onion, halved, sliced

1 garlic clove, minced

1 lb. boneless skinless chicken thighs

1½ teaspoons lemon-pepper seasoning

½ teaspoon dried oregano leaves

¼ teaspoon allspice

4 pita bread

½ cup plain yogurt

1 Italian plum tomato, sliced

½ medium cucumber, chopped (about ½ cup)

1. In 4- to 6-quart slow cooker, combine onion, garlic, chicken thighs, lemon-pepper seasoning, oregano and allspice; mix to coat chicken with seasoning.

2. Cover; cook on low setting for 6 to 8 hours.

3. About 10 minutes before serving, heat pita bread as directed on package. Meanwhile, remove chicken from slow cooker; place on large plate. Stir yogurt into onion mixture in slow cooker. Shred chicken with 2 forks. Spoon chicken onto warm pita breads. With slotted spoon, transfer onion mixture onto chicken; top with tomato and cucumber. Fold each pita bread in half.

NUTRITION INFORMATION PER SERVING: Serving Size: 1 Sandwich • Calories 390 • Calories from Fat 90 • % Daily Value: Total Fat 10g 15% • Saturated Fat 3g 15% • Cholesterol 75mg 25% • Sodium 680mg 28% • Total Carbohydrate 47g 16% • Dietary Fiber 3g 12% • Sugars 4g • Protein 29g • Vitamin A 4% • Vitamin C 6% • Calcium 15% • Iron 20% • **DIETARY EXCHANGES:** 3 Starch, 3 Lean Meat **OR** 3 Carbohydrate, 3 Lean Meat

DOUGHBOY TIP

If you don't have lemon-pepper seasoning, substitute ¾ teaspoon salt, ¼ teaspoon pepper and 1 teaspoon grated lemon peel.

hot turkey sandwiches

YIELD: 12 SANDWICHES

Prep Time: 15 minutes (Ready in 8 hours 15 minutes)

2 (2- to 2½-lb.) boneless turkey breast halves

½ teaspoon salt

½ teaspoon pepper

1 (10¾-oz.) can condensed cream of chicken soup

12 wheat or white sandwich buns, split

Cranberry sauce, if desired

1. Spray 3½- to 4-quart slow cooker with nonstick cooking spray. Place turkey breast halves in sprayed slow cooker. Sprinkle with salt and pepper.

2. Cover; cook on low setting for 7 to 8 hours.

3. About 10 minutes before serving, remove turkey from slow cooker; cool slightly. Remove ⅔ cup juices from slow cooker; place in small saucepan. Add soup; mix well. Cook over medium heat for about 5 minutes or until thoroughly heated, stirring occasionally. Meanwhile, cut turkey into slices; place on bottom halves of buns.

4. Pour gravy over turkey. Cover with top halves of buns. Serve sandwiches with cranberry sauce.

NUTRITION INFORMATION PER SERVING: Serving Size: 1 Sandwich • Calories 310 • Calories from Fat 45 • % Daily Value: Total Fat 5g 8% • Saturated Fat 1g 5% • Cholesterol 125mg 42% • Sodium 480mg 20% • Total Carbohydrate 20g 7% • Dietary Fiber 2g 8% • Sugars 2g • Protein 48g • Vitamin A 2% • Vitamin C 0% • Calcium 6% • Iron 20% • **DIETARY EXCHANGES:** 1 Starch, 6 Very Lean Meat **OR** 1 Carbohydrate, 6 Very Lean Meat

MAKE IT SPECIAL

This juicy turkey and flavorful gravy makes a "meal-in-one" open-faced sandwich. Bake a can of refrigerated buttermilk flaky biscuits and, while they're in the oven, cook a package of frozen broccoli spears. For each serving, place warm split biscuit halves on a plate, and top with a couple slices of turkey. Divide the broccoli among the biscuits, and spoon the gravy over all. Sprinkle with shredded Swiss cheese and, if you like, a few toasted sliced almonds.

tex-mex wraps with turkey

YIELD: 16 SANDWICHES

Prep Time: 15 minutes (Ready in 8 hours 15 minutes)

2 lb. turkey breast tenderloins

¼ teaspoon seasoned salt

¼ teaspoon pepper

½ cup chopped onion

⅓ cup water

2 (1.25-oz.) pkg. taco seasoning mix

16 (8- to 10-inch) flour tortillas

2 cups bite-sized pieces lettuce

8 oz. (2 cups) shredded Cheddar cheese

1. Place turkey breast tenderloins in 3½- to 4-quart slow cooker. Sprinkle with seasoned salt and pepper. Add onion and water.

2. Cover; cook on low setting for 6 to 7 hours.

3. About 1 hour 10 minutes before serving, remove turkey from slow cooker; place on large plate. Shred turkey with 2 forks.

4. Measure liquid from slow cooker; add enough water to liquid to measure 2 cups. Return liquid to slow cooker. Add taco seasoning mix; mix well. Stir in shredded turkey. Cover; cook on low setting an additional 1 hour.

5. Spoon about ¼ cup turkey onto center of each tortilla. Top each with lettuce and cheese; roll up.

NUTRITION INFORMATION PER SERVING: Serving Size: 1 Sandwich • Calories 260 • Calories from Fat 70 • % Daily Value: Total Fat 8g 12% • Saturated Fat 4g 20% • Cholesterol 50mg 17% • Sodium 520mg 22% • Total Carbohydrate 28g 9% • Dietary Fiber 2g 8% • Sugars 3g • Protein 21g • Vitamin A 10% • Vitamin C 2% • Calcium 14% • Iron 14% • **DIETARY EXCHANGES:** 2 Starch, 2 Lean Meat **OR** 2 Carbohydrate, 2 Lean Meat

DOUGHBOY TIP

If you're making these wraps to go, you can bring the turkey in the slow cooker. Pack the lettuce, tortillas and cheese in separate containers, and let guests make their own sandwiches on site. If there's electricity at the site, plug in the cooker and set it on low, otherwise serve the sandwiches within an hour.

georgia-style barbecued turkey sandwiches

YIELD: 12 SANDWICHES

Prep Time: 15 minutes (Ready in 10 hours 15 minutes)

4 turkey thighs (about 3 lb.), skin removed

½ cup firmly packed brown sugar

¼ cup prepared mustard

2 tablespoons ketchup

2 tablespoons cider vinegar

2 tablespoons Louisiana-style hot pepper sauce

1 teaspoon salt

1 teaspoon coarsely ground black pepper

1 teaspoon crushed red pepper flakes

2 teaspoons liquid smoke

12 sandwich buns, split

½ pint (1 cup) creamy coleslaw (from deli)

1. Spray 4- to 6-quart slow cooker with nonstick cooking spray. Place turkey thighs in sprayed slow cooker. In small bowl, combine all remaining ingredients except buns and coleslaw; mix well. Pour over turkey, turning turkey as necessary to coat.

2. Cover; cook on low setting for 8 to 10 hours.

3. About 10 minutes before serving, remove turkey from slow cooker; place on large plate. Remove meat from bones; discard bones. Shred turkey with 2 forks; return to slow cooker and mix well. With slotted spoon, spoon about ⅓ cup turkey mixture onto bottom halves of buns. Top each with rounded tablespoon coleslaw. Cover with top halves of buns.

NUTRITION INFORMATION PER SERVING: Serving Size: 1 Sandwich • Calories 260 • Calories from Fat 50 • % Daily Value: Total Fat 6g 9% • Saturated Fat 2g 10% • Cholesterol 45mg 15% • Sodium 560mg 23% • Total Carbohydrate 33g 11% • Dietary Fiber 2g 8% • Sugars 15g • Protein 18g • Vitamin A 4% • Vitamin C 4% • Calcium 10% • Iron 15% • **DIETARY EXCHANGES:** 1 Starch, 1 Fruit, 2 Lean Meat **OR** 2 Carbohydrate, 2 Lean Meat

DOUGHBOY TIP

Toasting warms the buns and prevents juices from soaking into the bread and making it soggy. Toast the cut sides of the buns under a broiler just before serving.

italian ground turkey rolls

YIELD: 12 SANDWICHES

Prep Time: 15 minutes (Ready in 2 hours 15 minutes)

2½ lb. lean ground turkey

½ cup chopped onion

3 to 4 garlic cloves, minced

1 (48-oz.) jar chunky garden vegetable tomato pasta sauce

1 (6-oz.) can tomato paste

12 (6-inch) French rolls, split

6 (1½-oz.) slices mozzarella cheese, halved

1. Spray large nonstick skillet with nonstick cooking spray. Heat over medium-high heat until hot. Add ground turkey, onion and garlic; cook 6 to 8 minutes or until turkey is well browned, stirring frequently. Drain.

2. In 3½- to 4-quart slow cooker, combine cooked turkey mixture, pasta sauce and tomato paste; mix well.

3. Cover; cook on low setting for 4 to 5 hours or on high setting for 2 hours.

4. Spoon ½ cup turkey mixture onto bottom halves of rolls. Top each with half slice of cheese, cutting to fit. Cover with top halves of rolls.

NUTRITION INFORMATION PER SERVING: Serving Size: 1 Sandwich • Calories 440 • Calories from Fat 135 • % Daily Value: Total Fat 15g 23% • Saturated Fat 5g 25% • Cholesterol 75mg 25% • Sodium 1110mg 46% • Total Carbohydrate 48g 16% • Dietary Fiber 4g 16% • Sugars 9g • Protein 32g • Vitamin A 24% • Vitamin C 18% • Calcium 22% • Iron 18% • **DIETARY EXCHANGES:** 3 Starch, 3 Lean Meat **OR** 3 Carbohydrate, 3 Lean Meat

SERVE WITH

These hearty sandwiches are great for toting to a potluck, company lunch or family get-together. Be sure to bring along the chips and tangy relishes such as pepperoncini peppers and crunchy pickle spears. Brownies or apple bars are an easy and great dessert.

bbq veggie joes

YIELD: 10 SANDWICHES

Prep Time: 30 minutes (Ready in 12 hours 30 minutes)

1 cup dried lentils, sorted, rinsed

2 cups water

1½ cups chopped celery

1½ cups chopped carrots

1 cup chopped onions

¾ cup ketchup

2 tablespoons dark brown sugar

2 tablespoons Worcestershire sauce

2 tablespoons cider vinegar

10 sesame seed buns, split, toasted

1. In medium saucepan, combine lentils and water. Bring to a boil. Reduce heat; cover and simmer 10 minutes.

2. Meanwhile, in 3½- to 4-quart slow cooker, combine celery, carrots, onions, ketchup, brown sugar and Worcestershire sauce; mix well. Stir in lentils with water.

3. Cover; cook on low setting for 10 to 12 hours. Stir in vinegar. Spoon ½ cup filling into each toasted bun.

NUTRITION INFORMATION PER SERVING: Serving Size: 1 Sandwich • Calories 250 • Calories from Fat 25 • % Daily Value: Total Fat 3g 5% • Saturated Fat 1g 5% • Cholesterol 0mg 0% • Sodium 510mg 21% • Total Carbohydrate 45g 15% • Dietary Fiber 8g 32% • Sugars 12g • Protein 10g • Vitamin A 110% • Vitamin C 10% • Calcium 10% • Iron 20% • **DIETARY EXCHANGES:** 2½ Starch, ½ Fruit, ½ Very Lean Meat **OR** 3 Carbohydrate, ½ Very Lean Meat

DOUGHBOY TIP

A food processor makes quick work of chopping the vegetables for these sandwiches. Two carrots, two stalks of celery and one large onion will give you the measured amounts.

very easy vegetables and sides

Old-Fashioned Baked Beans 156

Savory Red Beans and Rice 157

Tex-Mex Baked Beans 158

White Beans with Sun-Dried Tomatoes 159

Spicy Black-Eyed Peas 160

Creamy Wild Rice 161

Vegetable-Rice Pilaf 162

Herbed Wild Rice Pilaf 163

Couscous-Stuffed Peppers 164

Easy Scalloped Corn 165

Alfredo Green Bean Casserole 166

Ginger Squash 167

Garlic Smashed Red Potatoes 168

Au Gratin Potatoes and Onion 169

Chile-Cheese Party Potatoes 170

Peachy Glazed Sweet Potatoes 171

OLD-FASHIONED BAKED BEANS, PAGE 156

old-fashioned baked beans

YIELD: 20 SERVINGS

Prep Time: 10 minutes (Ready in 38 hours 10 minutes)

2 (16-oz.) pkg. (2⅓ cups each) dried navy beans, sorted, rinsed

9 cups water

⅔ cup firmly packed brown sugar

⅔ cup molasses

1 tablespoon prepared mustard

1 teaspoon salt

1 cup chopped onions

1. In 4- to 6-quart slow cooker, combine beans and water.

2. Cover; cook on high setting for 2 hours.

3. Turn off slow cooker. Let beans stand 8 to 24 hours.

4. Stir in all remaining ingredients. Reduce heat setting to low; cover and cook an additional 10 to 12 hours or until beans are very tender and most of liquid is absorbed.

NUTRITION INFORMATION PER SERVING: Serving Size: ½₀ of Recipe • Calories 190 • Calories from Fat 10 • % Daily Value: Total Fat 1g 2% • Saturated Fat 0g 0% • Cholesterol 0mg 0% • Sodium 135mg 6% • Total Carbohydrate 43g 14% • Dietary Fiber 7g 28% • Sugars 17g • Protein 9g • Vitamin A 0% • Vitamin C 0% • Calcium 10% • Iron 18% • **DIETARY EXCHANGES:** 2½ Starch **OR** 3 Carbohydrate

SERVE WITH

Baked beans are a true summertime favorite. When the heat is on, pack up a picnic of deli fried chicken, large biscuits and these slow-cooked beans. Put the chicken in a cooler with a pint of potato salad and juicy watermelon slices before heading off to your picnic or party site.

savory red beans and rice

YIELD: 16 SERVINGS

Prep Time: 15 minutes (Ready in 5 hours 35 minutes)

1 (16-oz.) pkg. (2½ cups) dried kidney beans, sorted, rinsed

1 large green bell pepper, chopped (1½ cups)

1 cup chopped onions

2 garlic cloves, minced

7 cups water

1½ teaspoons salt

¼ teaspoon pepper

2 cups uncooked instant rice

Hot pepper sauce, if desired

1. In 3½- to 6-quart slow cooker, combine all ingredients except rice; mix well.

2. Cover; cook on high setting for 4 to 5 hours.

3. Stir rice into bean mixture. Cover; cook on high setting an additional 15 to 20 minutes or until rice is tender. Serve beans and rice with hot pepper sauce.

NUTRITION INFORMATION PER SERVING: Serving Size: ¹⁄₁₆ of Recipe • Calories 125 • Calories from Fat 0 • % Daily Value: Total Fat 0g 0% • Saturated Fat 0g 0% • Cholesterol 0mg 0% • Sodium 220mg 9% • Total Carbohydrate 29g 10% • Dietary Fiber 5g 20% • Sugars 1g • Protein 7g • Vitamin A 0% • Vitamin C 8% • Calcium 2% • Iron 14% • **DIETARY EXCHANGES:** 2 Starch, 2 Vegetable **OR** 2 Carbohydrate, 2 Vegetable

SERVE WITH

What kid or "grown-up kid" doesn't love **Crescent Dogs?** Heat oven to 375°F. Cut 4 slices American cheese into 6 strips each. Cut lengthwise slits in 8 hot dogs to within ½ inch of ends. Insert 3 strips of cheese into each slit. Separate an 8-oz. can refrigerated crescent dinner rolls into 8 triangles. Place a hot dog on each wide end of triangle; roll as directed on can. Place on ungreased cookie sheet with cheese side up. Bake 12 to 15 minutes or until golden brown.

tex-mex baked beans

YIELD: 14 SERVINGS

Prep Time: 10 minutes (Ready in 4 hours 10 minutes)

2 (15.5-oz.) cans great northern beans, drained, rinsed

2 (15-oz.) cans black beans, drained, rinsed

1 (8-oz.) can tomato sauce

1 (4.5-oz.) can chopped green chiles

¾ cup barbecue sauce

¾ cup chunky-style salsa

¼ cup firmly packed brown sugar

1. In 3½- or 4-quart slow cooker, combine all ingredients; mix well.

2. Cover; cook on low setting for at least 4 hours.

NUTRITION INFORMATION PER SERVING: Serving Size: ¹⁄₁₄ of Recipe • Calories 130 • Calories from Fat 10 • % Daily Value: Total Fat 1g 2% • Saturated Fat 0g 0% • Cholesterol 0mg 0% • Sodium 550mg 23% • Total Carbohydrate 24g 8% • Dietary Fiber 6g 24% • Sugars 6g • Protein 6g • Vitamin A 6% • Vitamin C 6% • Calcium 8% • Iron 10% • **DIETARY EXCHANGES:** 1 Starch, ½ Fruit, ½ Very Lean Meat **OR** 1½ Carbohydrate, ½ Very Lean Meat

KIDS CAN HELP

Let the kids "hide" the hot dog in these **Corn Dogs.** Heat oven to 350°F. Separate a 17.3-oz. can large refrigerated golden corn biscuits or a 16.3-oz. can large refrigerated buttermilk biscuits into 8 biscuits. Press each into 6½-inch oval. Spread each oval with 1 teaspoon ketchup and 1 teaspoon prepared mustard. Place a hot dog in center of each biscuit. Roll dough around hot dog; seal ends and edges well. Place seam side down on greased cookie sheet. Bake 15 to 18 minutes or until golden brown.

white beans with sun-dried tomatoes

YIELD: 10 SERVINGS

Prep Time: 10 minutes (Ready in 5 hours 10 minutes)

1 (16-oz.) pkg. (2⅓ cups) dried great northern beans, sorted, rinsed

2 garlic cloves, minced

6 cups water

1½ teaspoons dried basil leaves

1 teaspoon salt

¼ teaspoon pepper

¾ cup finely chopped sun-dried tomatoes in olive oil

1 (2¼-oz.) can sliced ripe olives, drained

1. In 3½- to 6-quart slow cooker, combine all ingredients except tomatoes and olives; mix well.

2. Cover; cook on high setting for 4 to 5 hours. Stir tomatoes and olives into bean mixture before serving.

NUTRITION INFORMATION PER SERVING: Serving Size: 1/10 of Recipe • Calories 155 • Calories from Fat 20 • % Daily Value: Total Fat 2g 3% • Saturated Fat 0g 0% • Cholesterol 0mg 0% • Sodium 320mg 13% • Total Carbohydrate 31g 10% • Dietary Fiber 8g 32% • Sugars 2g • Protein 11g • Vitamin A 2% • Vitamin C 6% • Calcium 10% • Iron 26% • **DIETARY EXCHANGES:** 2 Starch **OR** 2 Carbohydrate

SERVE WITH

Warm **Onion Pepper Biscuits** and crisp carrot, celery and green bell pepper sticks complete this meal. Heat oven to 375°F. Separate a 12-oz. can refrigerated flaky biscuits into 10 biscuits; place on ungreased cookie sheet. Cook 3 tablespoons finely chopped onion in 1 tablespoon margarine until tender. Divide onion mixture among biscuits; spread evenly. Sprinkle with coarsely ground black pepper. Bake 15 to 20 minutes or until golden brown.

spicy black-eyed peas

YIELD: 8 SERVINGS

Prep Time: 15 minutes (Ready in 4 hours 15 minutes)

1 (16-oz.) pkg. (2⅓ cups) dried black-eyed peas, sorted, rinsed

½ cup chopped onion

6 cups water

1 teaspoon salt

½ teaspoon pepper

¾ cup chunky-style salsa

1. In 3½- to 6-quart slow cooker, combine all ingredients except salsa; mix well.

2. Cover; cook on high setting for 3 to 4 hours.

3. About 10 minutes before serving, stir salsa into bean mixture. Cover; cook on high setting an additional 5 to 10 minutes or until thoroughly heated.

NUTRITION INFORMATION PER SERVING: Serving Size: ⅛ of Recipe • Calories 145 • Calories from Fat 10 • % Daily Value: Total Fat 1g 2% • Saturated Fat 0g 0% • Cholesterol 0mg 0% • Sodium 410mg 17% • Total Carbohydrate 35g 12% • Dietary Fiber 11g 44% • Sugars 4g • Protein 13g • Vitamin A 2% • Vitamin C 4% • Calcium 4% • Iron 22% • **DIETARY EXCHANGES:** 1 Starch, 4 Vegetable **OR** 2½ Carbohydrate, 4 Vegetable

MAKE IT SPECIAL
Top each serving with a dollop of sour cream and a big spoonful of salsa. Hot salsa goes well with the black-eyed peas, but you can use medium or mild if your family likes a milder taste.

creamy wild rice

YIELD: 12 SERVINGS
Prep Time: 15 minutes (Ready in 9 hours 15 minutes)

1½ cups uncooked wild rice

½ cup chopped onion

½ teaspoon salt

½ teaspoon ground sage

¼ teaspoon pepper

1 (10¾-oz.) can condensed cream of celery soup

1 (10¾-oz.) can condensed cream of mushroom soup

2¼ cups water

¼ cup chopped fresh parsley

1. Rinse rice with cold water; drain. In 5- to 6-quart slow cooker, combine rice and all remaining ingredients except parsley; mix well.

2. Cover; cook on low setting for 8 to 9 hours. Stir parsley into rice mixture before serving.

NUTRITION INFORMATION PER SERVING: Serving Size: ½₁₂ of Recipe • Calories 125 • Calories from Fat 25 • % Daily Value: Total Fat 3g 5% • Saturated Fat 1g 5% • Cholesterol 0mg 0% • Sodium 460mg 19% • Total Carbohydrate 21g 7% • Dietary Fiber 2g 8% • Sugars 2g • Protein 4g • Vitamin A 4% • Vitamin C 2% • Calcium 2% • Iron 4% • **DIETARY EXCHANGES:** 1½ Starch **OR** 1½ Carbohydrate

MAKE IT SPECIAL
To add crunch and flavor to this creamy dish, add a couple tablespoons of toasted pecans or almonds. You can either stir them in or sprinkle them right on top.

vegetable-rice pilaf

YIELD: 12 SERVINGS

Prep Time: 10 minutes (Ready in 2 hours 10 minutes)

1 (14-oz.) can chicken broth with roasted garlic

⅔ cup water

1½ cups uncooked converted long-grain white rice

1 tablespoon olive oil

1¼ cups frozen cut green beans

½ cup sliced carrot

2 green onions, sliced

½ teaspoon salt

¼ teaspoon lemon-pepper seasoning

1. In 4-cup microwave-safe measuring cup, combine broth and water. Microwave on HIGH for 4 to 5 minutes or until steaming hot.

2. Meanwhile, spray 4- to 6-quart slow cooker with nonstick cooking spray. Combine rice and oil in sprayed slow cooker; mix well. Add all remaining ingredients and hot broth mixture.

3. Cover; cook on high setting for 1½ to 2 hours.

NUTRITION INFORMATION PER SERVING: Serving Size: ¹⁄₁₂ of Recipe • Calories 110 • Calories from Fat 20 • % Daily Value: Total Fat 2g 3% • Saturated Fat 0g 0% • Cholesterol 0mg 0% • Sodium 120mg 5% • Total Carbohydrate 21g 7% • Dietary Fiber 1g 4% • Sugars 1g • Protein 2g • Vitamin A 30% • Vitamin C 2% • Calcium 2% • Iron 6% • **DIETARY EXCHANGES:** 1½ Starch **OR** 2½ Carbohydrate

DOUGHBOY TIP

A helpful rice rule for this recipe is to use converted rice. Converted rice is processed to keep the grains from becoming sticky when cooked. To keep this dish warm, set the slow cooker on low for up to 2 hours.

herbed wild rice pilaf

YIELD: 12 SERVINGS

Prep Time: 10 minutes (Ready in 5 hours 10 minutes)

1½ cups uncooked wild rice

½ cup sliced green onions

1 (4.5-oz.) jar sliced mushrooms, drained

1 garlic clove, minced

¾ teaspoon salt

1 (14-oz.) can chicken broth

2 cups water

½ cup dried cherries

¾ teaspoon dried thyme leaves

¼ teaspoon nutmeg

2 tablespoons chopped fresh parsley

1. Spray 4- to 6-quart slow cooker with nonstick cooking spray. Rinse rice with cold water; drain. In sprayed slow cooker, combine rice, onions, mushrooms, garlic, salt, broth and water; stir gently to mix.

2. Cover; cook on high setting for 3 to 4 hours.

3. About 1 hour before serving, stir cherries, thyme and nutmeg into rice mixture. Reduce heat setting to low; cover and cook an additional 30 to 60 minutes or until rice is opened and tender. Stir parsley into rice pilaf before serving.

NUTRITION INFORMATION PER SERVING: Serving Size: ¹⁄₁₂ of Recipe • Calories 110 • Calories from Fat 10 • % Daily Value: Total Fat 1g 2% • Saturated Fat 0g 0% • Cholesterol 0mg 0% • Sodium 180mg 8% • Total Carbohydrate 21g 7% • Dietary Fiber 2g 8% • Sugars 4g • Protein 4g • Vitamin A 6% • Vitamin C 0% • Calcium 0% • Iron 4% • **DIETARY EXCHANGES:** 1 Starch, ½ Fruit **OR** 1½ Carbohydrate

DOUGHBOY TIP

Don't forget to wash your wild rice before cooking it. Place the rice in a bowl of cold water, and swirl it around with your hand. When the water becomes cloudy, drain the rice. Repeat the process until the water remains clear.

couscous-stuffed peppers

YIELD: 4 SERVINGS

Prep Time: 20 minutes (Ready in 7 hours 20 minutes)

4 large bell peppers

½ cup chopped onion

1 large garlic clove, minced

1 (15-oz.) can tomato sauce

½ teaspoon cumin

¼ teaspoon salt

¼ teaspoon cinnamon

⅛ teaspoon ground red pepper (cayenne)

1 cup uncooked couscous

¾ cup water

Pine nuts, if desired

Chopped fresh cilantro, if desired

1. Cut thin slice from stem end of each bell pepper to remove top of pepper. Remove seeds and membranes; rinse peppers.

2. In large skillet, cook onion and garlic over medium heat for about 5 minutes, stirring occasionally. Drain. Add tomato sauce, cumin, salt, cinnamon and ground red pepper; mix well. Stir in couscous. Divide mixture evenly into bell peppers.

3. Pour water into 4½- to 6-quart slow cooker. Stand bell peppers upright in cooker.

4. Cover; cook on low setting for 5 to 7 hours. Sprinkle pine nuts and cilantro onto stuffed peppers before serving.

NUTRITION INFORMATION PER SERVING: Serving Size: ¼ of Recipe • Calories 235 • Calories from Fat 10 • % Daily Value: Total Fat 1g 2% • Saturated Fat 0g 0% • Cholesterol 0mg 0% • Sodium 850mg 35% • Total Carbohydrate 54g 18% • Dietary Fiber 7g 28% • Sugars 10g • Protein 9g • Vitamin A 28% • Vitamin C 100% • Calcium 4% • Iron 12% • **DIETARY EXCHANGES:** 2 Starch, 2 Vegetable, 1 High-Fat Meat **OR** 2 Carbohydrate, 2 Vegetable, 1 High-Fat Meat

SERVE WITH

Pasta-filled peppers are a welcome change from the standard veggie choices. You can't go wrong with choosing lamb, pork or chicken to pair with this unusually delicious side dish.

easy scalloped corn

YIELD: 8 SERVINGS
Prep Time: 15 minutes (Ready in 3 hours 15 minutes)

²⁄₃ cup all-purpose flour

¼ cup margarine or butter, melted

1 (8-oz.) carton (1 cup) refrigerated or frozen fat-free egg product, thawed

¾ cup evaporated milk

2 teaspoons sugar

1 teaspoon salt

⅛ teaspoon pepper

1 (14.75-oz.) can cream-style corn

1 (15.25-oz.) can whole kernel corn, drained

1. Spray 2- to 4-quart slow cooker with nonstick cooking spray. In large bowl, combine all ingredients except whole kernel corn; mix well. Stir in whole kernel corn. Pour into sprayed slow cooker.

2. Cover; cook on high setting for 2 to 3 hours.

NUTRITION INFORMATION PER SERVING: Serving Size: ⅛ of Recipe • Calories 220 • Calories from Fat 70 • % Daily Value: Total Fat 8g 12% • Saturated Fat 2g 10% • Cholesterol 5mg 2% • Sodium 670mg 28% • Total Carbohydrate 32g 11% • Dietary Fiber 3g 12% • Sugars 7g • Protein 8g • Vitamin A 16% • Vitamin C 16% • Calcium 8% • Iron 10% • **DIETARY EXCHANGES:** 2 Starch, ½ Fat **OR** 2 Carbohydrate, ½ Fat

SERVE WITH

For a Southern-style supper, serve this scalloped corn with a drizzle of maple syrup, along with slices of baked ham and warm-from-the-oven large buttermilk biscuits. Lemonade or iced tea with a twist of lemon and few sprigs of mint is a refreshing beverage.

alfredo green bean casserole

YIELD: 10 SERVINGS

Prep Time: 10 minutes (Ready in 4 hours 10 minutes)

1 (28-oz.) pkg. frozen cut green beans

1 (8-oz.) can sliced water chestnuts, drained

½ cup roasted red bell pepper strips (from a jar)

¼ teaspoon salt

1 (10-oz.) container refrigerated Alfredo sauce

1 (2.8-oz.) can french fried onions

1. In 4- to 6-quart slow cooker, combine all ingredients except onions. Stir in half of the onions.

2. Cover; cook on high setting for 3 to 4 hours, stirring after 1 to 1½ hours.

3. About 5 minutes before serving, in small skillet, heat remaining half of onions over medium-high heat for 2 to 3 minutes or until hot, stirring frequently. Stir bean mixture; sprinkle with onions.

NUTRITION INFORMATION PER SERVING: Serving Size: ¹⁄₁₀ of Recipe • Calories 180 • Calories from Fat 125 • % Daily Value: Total Fat 14g 22% • Saturated Fat 7g 35% • Cholesterol 30mg 10% • Sodium 260mg 11% • Total Carbohydrate 13g 4% • Dietary Fiber 3g 12% • Sugars 3g • Protein 4g • Vitamin A 22% • Vitamin C 12% • Calcium 12% • Iron 6% • **DIETARY EXCHANGES:** 2½ Vegetable, 2½ Fat

SERVE WITH

Oh-so-easy and oh-so-popular, this holiday-ready dish shines when served with **Garlic Herb Biscuits.** Separate a 16.3-oz. can large refrigerated buttermilk biscuits into 8 biscuits. Brush top and sides of each biscuit with melted margarine; coat with ¼ cup garlic herb bread crumbs. Bake as directed on can.

ginger squash

YIELD: 4 SERVINGS

Prep Time: 15 minutes (Ready in 4 hours 15 minutes)

2 (¾-lb.) acorn squash

¼ cup water

¼ cup firmly packed brown sugar

¼ cup margarine or butter, melted

3 tablespoons dry sherry or apple juice

1½ teaspoons ginger

¼ teaspoon salt

1. Cut squash in half crosswise; remove seeds and membranes.

2. Pour water into 5- to 6-quart slow cooker. Place squash halves, cut sides up, in slow cooker. If necessary, stack squash halves in slow cooker so they fit. In small bowl, combine all remaining ingredients; mix well. Spoon into squash halves.

3. Cover; cook on high setting for 3 to 4 hours.

NUTRITION INFORMATION PER SERVING: Serving Size: ¼ of Recipe • Calories 295 • Calories from Fat 110 • % Daily Value: Total Fat 12g 18% • Saturated Fat 7g 35% • Cholesterol 30mg 10% • Sodium 240mg 10% • Total Carbohydrate 46g 15% • Dietary Fiber 3g 12% • Sugars 17g • Protein 3g • Vitamin A 24% • Vitamin C 18% • Calcium 10% • Iron 12% • **DIETARY EXCHANGES:** 1 Starch, 2 Fruit, 2 Fat **OR** 3 Carbohydrate, 2 Fat

MAKE IT SPECIAL

For a scrumptious side dish full of fall harvest flair, fill the squash with chopped crisp red apples and coarsely chopped toasted walnuts. Just add them to the sauce in the centers of the squash halves. Right before serving, sprinkle chopped crystallized ginger around the edges of the squash for added flavor.

garlic smashed red potatoes

YIELD: 14 SERVINGS

Prep Time: 15 minutes (Ready in 4 hours 45 minutes)

3 lb. small (2- to 3-inch) red potatoes

4 garlic cloves, minced

2 tablespoons olive oil

1 teaspoon salt

½ cup water

½ cup cream cheese with chives and onions (from 8-oz. container)

¼ to ½ cup milk

1. Halve or quarter potatoes as necessary to make similar-sized pieces. Place in 4- to 6-quart slow cooker. Add garlic, oil, salt and water; mix well to coat all potato pieces.

2. Cover; cook on high setting for 3½ to 4½ hours.

3. With fork or potato masher, mash potatoes and garlic. Add cream cheese; stir until well blended. Stir in enough milk for soft serving consistency. Serve immediately, or cover and let stand on low setting up to 1 hour.

NUTRITION INFORMATION PER SERVING: Serving Size: ⅟14 of Recipe • Calories 140 • Calories from Fat 45 • % Daily Value: Total Fat 5g 8% • Saturated Fat 2g 10% • Cholesterol 10mg 3% • Sodium 190mg 8% • Total Carbohydrate 21g 7% • Dietary Fiber 2g 8% • Sugars 1g • Protein 3g • Vitamin A 2% • Vitamin C 10% • Calcium 2% • Iron 6% • **DIETARY EXCHANGES:** 1½ Starch, ½ Fat **OR** 1½ Carbohydrate, ½ Fat

DOUGHBOY TIP

Next time you are in charge of bringing the mashed potatoes to a family gathering, prepare this recipe. Wrap the slow cooker in several layers of towels to keep it warm. Use rubber bands or kitchen string around the handles to keep the lid in place during the trip. When you arrive, plug in the cooker and set it on low to keep the potatoes warm until it's time to serve them.

au gratin potatoes and onion

YIELD: 14 SERVINGS

Prep Time: 15 minutes (Ready in 9 hours 15 minutes)

6 cups (6 medium) sliced peeled potatoes

½ cup coarsely chopped onion

4 oz. (1 cup) shredded American cheese

*1 (10¾-oz.) can condensed 98% fat-free cream of mushroom soup
with 30% less sodium*

½ cup milk

¼ to ½ teaspoon dried thyme leaves

1. In 3½- to 4-quart slow cooker, layer half each of the potatoes, onion and cheese; repeat layers. In small bowl, combine soup, milk and thyme; mix well. Pour over top.

2. Cover; cook on high setting for 1 hour.

3. Reduce heat setting to low; cover and cook an additional 6 to 8 hours.

NUTRITION INFORMATION PER SERVING: Serving Size: ⅟₁₄ of Recipe • Calories 90 • Calories from Fat 25 • % Daily Value: Total Fat 3g 5% • Saturated Fat 2g 10% • Cholesterol 10mg 3% • Sodium 140mg 6% • Total Carbohydrate 13g 4% • Dietary Fiber 1g 4% • Sugars 2g • Protein 4g • Vitamin A 2% • Vitamin C 4% • Calcium 6% • Iron 2% • **DIETARY EXCHANGES:** 1 Starch, ½ Fat **OR** 1 Carbohydrate, ½ Fat

MAKE IT SPECIAL

Make a marvelous main meal out of this potato dish by adding 1½ cups of cubed cooked ham. Layer the ham in the slow cooker after you've added the onion.

VERY EASY VEGETABLES AND SIDES **169**

chile-cheese party potatoes

YIELD: 12 SERVINGS

Prep Time: 10 minutes (Ready in 4 hours 40 minutes)

1 (10¾-oz.) can condensed cream of mushroom soup

1 (8-oz.) container sour cream

1 (4.5-oz.) can chopped green chiles

6 oz. (1½ cups) shredded colby-Monterey Jack cheese blend

1 (32-oz.) pkg. frozen southern-style cubed hash-brown potatoes

3 green onions, sliced

½ cup finely crushed nacho-flavored taco chips

1. Spray 4- to 6-quart slow cooker with nonstick cooking spray. In medium bowl, combine soup, sour cream, chiles and cheese; mix well.

2. Arrange half of potatoes in sprayed slow cooker. Top with half of sour cream mixture; spread evenly. Top with remaining potatoes and sour cream mixture; spread evenly.

3. Cover; cook on high setting for 3½ to 4½ hours. Sprinkle onions and chips onto potato mixture before serving.

NUTRITION INFORMATION PER SERVING: Serving Size: ¹⁄₁₂ of Recipe • Calories 200 • Calories from Fat 100 • % Daily Value: Total Fat 11g 17% • Saturated Fat 6g 30% • Cholesterol 25mg 8% • Sodium 370mg 15% • Total Carbohydrate 19g 6% • Dietary Fiber 2g 8% • Sugars 2g • Protein 7g • Vitamin A 10% • Vitamin C 10% • Calcium 15% • Iron 6% • **DIETARY EXCHANGES:** 1½ Starch, ½ High-Fat Meat, 1 Fat **OR** 1½ Carbohydrate, ½ High-Fat Meat, 1 Fat

DOUGHBOY TIP

When you're scouting out hash browns, you'll find that the Southern-style hash-brown potatoes are cubed and the country-style hash browns are shredded. This recipe calls for cubed potatoes, but both styles work well.

peachy glazed sweet potatoes

YIELD: 10 SERVINGS

Prep Time: 15 minutes (Ready in 3 hours 45 minutes)

2¼ lb. dark-orange sweet potatoes, peeled

1 cup peach pie filling (from 21-oz. can)

2 tablespoons margarine or butter, melted

1 teaspoon grated gingerroot

¼ teaspoon salt

½ cup coarsely chopped pecans

2 tablespoons brown sugar

1 tablespoon margarine or butter

⅛ teaspoon cinnamon

1. Spray 4- to 6-quart slow cooker with nonstick cooking spray. Halve larger sweet potatoes lengthwise; cut each into ½-inch slices. Place in sprayed slow cooker. Add pie filling, 2 tablespoons melted margarine, gingerroot and salt; mix well to coat potatoes.

2. Cover; cook on high setting for 2½ to 3½ hours.

3. Meanwhile, line cookie sheet with foil. In small skillet, combine pecans, brown sugar, 1 tablespoon margarine and cinnamon; mix well. Cook over medium heat for 2 to 3 minutes or until bubbly and glazed, stirring frequently. Spoon pecan mixture onto foil-lined cookie sheet to cool.

4. Gently stir potatoes. Sprinkle pecan mixture onto sweet potatoes before serving.

NUTRITION INFORMATION PER SERVING: Serving Size: ¹⁄₁₀ of Recipe • Calories 200 • Calories from Fat 70 • % Daily Value: Total Fat 8g 12% • Saturated Fat 1g 5% • Cholesterol 0mg 0% • Sodium 110mg 5% • Total Carbohydrate 29g 10% • Dietary Fiber 3g 12% • Sugars 12g • Protein 2g • Vitamin A 360% • Vitamin C 25% • Calcium 2% • Iron 4% • **DIETARY EXCHANGES:** 1 Starch, 1 Fruit, 1½ Fat **OR** 2 Carbohydrate, 1½ Fat

DOUGHBOY TIP

Coating is the key to success when slow-cooking fresh sweet potatoes. The pie filling in this recipe glazes the potatoes so they don't turn brown. Plus, it adds a slightly sweet and fruity flavor. Feel free to use apricot pie filling in place of the peach filling.

index

Note: Pages in **bold** refer to photographs.

Alfredo Green Bean Casserole, 166, **166**
Au Gratin Potatoes and Onion, 169
Autumn Pork Roast Dinner, 36

Barbecued
  Beef Sandwiches, Easy, 133
  Ribs, Slow-and-Easy, 42, **42**
  Turkey and Vegetables, 82, **82**
  Turkey Sandwiches, Georgia-Style, 150, **151**
  Veggie Joes, 153
BBQ Veggie Joes, 153
Bean(s)
  Baked, Old-Fashioned, **154**, 156
  Baked, Tex-Mex, 158, **158**
  BBQ Veggie Joes, 153
  and Beef Tamale Pie, 26, **27**
  Black, Soup, Cuban, 97
  and Chicken Stew, Southwestern, 115, **115**
  Chili Beef and, 28
  Chili con Crescents, 28
  Green, Casserole, Alfredo, 166, **166**
  Ground Turkey and, 87, **87**
  Ham and Chicken Enchilada Casserole, 49
  lentils, types of, 124
  Mango Chutney-Chicken Curry, 57
  'n Wieners, 53
  Red, and Rice, Jambalaya with, 72
  Red, and Rice, Savory, 157
  soaking methods, 96
  Spicy Vegetarian Chili, 129
  Stew, Ratatouille, 125
  Texas Chili, **90**, 126, **126**
  and Turkey Cassoulet, 84
  Two-, Chili, Meaty, 128
  Vegetable, and Ham Soup, 96
  Vegetable, Lentil and Pasta Stew, 124
  Vegetable Minestrone Soup, 104
  White, with Sun-Dried Tomatoes, 159, **159**
Beef
  and Bean Tamale Pie, 26, **27**
  and Beans, Chili, 28
  Beans 'n Wieners, 53
  Beefy Tortilla Casserole, 30, **30**
  Brisket with Cranberry Gravy, 13
  Cajun Pot Roast with Corn and Tomatoes, 12

Caramelized Onion Pot Roast, 14, **15**
Cheeseburger Sandwiches, 139, **139**
Cheesy Italian Tortellini, 31, **31**
Chili con Crescents, 28
Corn Dogs, 158
Corned, and Cabbage, **18**, 19
Crescent Dogs, 157
Hamburger-Noodle Soup, 98, **98**
Hearty Steak and Tater Soup, 95, **95**
Hungarian Stew, 113
Meaty Two-Bean Chili, 128
Mediterranean Steak Roll, 20
Mexican Round Steak, 16
and Mushrooms, Burgundy, 23, **23**
Philly Cheese Steak Sandwiches, 135, **135**
Picadillo with Apples and Almonds, 29
Pitas, Creamy, 138, **138**
and Pork Chili, Chunky, 127, **127**
Ragout on Polenta, 22, **22**
Sandwiches, Double-Onion, 134, **134**
Sandwiches, Easy Barbecued, 133
Sandwiches, Southwest, 136
Sandwiches au Jus, Hot, 132
Saucy Pepper Steak, **10**, 17
Sauerbraten, 24
Sloppy Joe Shortcakes, 137
So-Easy Sloppy Joes, 137
Stew, Curried, 112
Stew, Family-Favorite, 114, **114**
Swiss Steak Stew, 109
Swiss Steak Supper, 21
Texas Chili, **90**, 126, **126**
and Tomatoes, Rosemary, 25
Veal Paprika, 32
Beefy Tortilla Casserole, 30, **30**
Biscuit Cups, 84
Biscuit Flat Breads, 52
Biscuit Sandwiches, Ham 'n' Cheese, 105
Biscuits, Garlic Cheese, 81
Biscuits, Garlic Herb, 166
Biscuits, Italian, 45
Biscuits, Smothered Buttermilk Chicken over, 74, **74**
Biscuits, Warm Onion Pepper, 159
Black-Eyed Peas, Spicy, 160
Bolognese Pasta Sauce with Spaghetti, 44
Bratwurst and Sauerkraut, 141
Breads
  Biscuit Cups, 84

Biscuit Flat Breads, 52
Cheddar Cheese Pull-Apart, 117
Cheese Bursts, 61
Cheesy Dill Crescents, 119
Chili con Crescents, 28
Chive Crescents, 48
Garlic Cheese Biscuits, 81
Garlic Herb Biscuits, 166
Italian Biscuits, 45
Lumpy Cheese Bread, 95
Onion 'n' Cream Crescents, 86
Parmesan Rosemary Crescents, 79
Soft Pretzels, 53
Warm Onion Pepper Biscuits, 159
Bulgur and Feta Cheese, Turkey Breast with, 80
Burgundy Beef and Mushrooms, 23, **23**
Burritos, Pulled-Pork, 142, **142**

Cabbage
  Bratwurst and Sauerkraut, 141
  Chicken, and Sausage Stew with Wild Rice, 117
  Corned Beef and, **18**, 19
  Gingered Pork Wraps, 140
  and Pork Soup, 92
Cajun Pot Roast with Corn and Tomatoes, 12
Cajun-Seasoned Chicken, 64
Caramelized Onion Pot Roast, 14, **15**
Cheddar Cheese Pull-Apart, 117
Cheese
  -Chile Party Potatoes, 170, **170**
  Au Gratin Potatoes and Onion, 169
  Beefy Tortilla Casserole, 30, **30**
  Biscuits, Garlic, 81
  Bread, Lumpy, 95
  Bursts, 61
  Cheddar, Pull-Apart, 117
  Cheeseburger Sandwiches, 139, **139**
  Cheesy Dill Crescents, 119
  Cheesy Italian Tortellini, 31, **31**
  French Onion Soup with Cheesy Bread, 108
  Ham and Chicken Enchilada Casserole, 49
  Italian Sausage Lasagna, **46**, 47
  'n' Ham Biscuit Sandwiches, 105
  Onion 'n' Cream Crescents, 86
  Open-Faced Pizza Sandwiches, 143, **143**
  Parmesan Rosemary Crescents, 79
  Pizza Pork Chops, 40
  Steak Sandwiches, Philly, 135, **135**

Cheeseburger Sandwiches, 139, **139**
Cheesy Dill Crescents, 119
Cheesy Italian Tortellini, 31, **31**
Chicken
    -Mango Chutney Curry, 57
    and Bean Stew, Southwestern, 115,
      115
    Breasts Supreme, 62, **62**
    Brunswick Stew, 121
    Cacciatore, Easy, **70**, 71
    Cajun-Seasoned, 64
    and Corn Soup, Mexicali, 100
    and Cornmeal Wedges, 73
    with Creamy Paprika Sauce, 68
    Drumsticks with Sweet Potatoes
      and Pineapple, 75, **75**
    Fettuccine Alfredo, 60
    Five-Spice, Big Bowls, 69
    and Ham Enchilada Casserole, 49
    Herbed, and Stuffing Supper, 56
    Italiano, 61
    Jambalaya with Red Beans and
      Rice, 72
    Jerked, Hoagies, 145
    Legs with Herbed Onion Sauce, 77
    Noodle Soup, Grandma's, 99, **99**
    Pita Folds, Greek, **146,** 147
    with Rice, Sweet-and-Sour, **54**, 76
    Salsa, 67, **67**
    Sausage, and Cabbage Stew with
      Wild Rice, 117
    Smothered Buttermilk, over
      Biscuits, 74, **74**
    Spanish, 63, **63**
    Stew, Moroccan, 120
    Stroganoff Pot Pie, 66, **66**
    Thai Peanut, 65
    in Wine Sauce, 58, **59**
Chile-Cheese Party Potatoes, 170, **170**
chiles, canned, buying, 115
Chili
    Beef and Beans, 28
    Chunky Beef and Pork, 127, **127**
    con Crescents, 28
    Meaty Two-Bean, 128
    Spicy Vegetarian, 129
    Texas, **90**, 126, **126**
Chive Crescents, 48
Chocolate-Filled Crescents, 120
Chop Suey, Easy Pork, 38, **38**
chorizo, about, 94
Chorizo, Yellow Pea Soup with, 94,
    94
Chowder, Dill-Turkey, 101
Chowder, Peppery Fish, 103, **103**
Chunky Beef and Pork Chili, 127, **127**
cilantro, about, 88
Corn, Easy Scalloped, 165
Corn and Chicken Soup, Mexicali,
    100
Corn and Tomatoes, Cajun Pot Roast
    with, 12

Corn Dogs, 158
Corned Beef and Cabbage, **18,** 19
Couscous-Stuffed Peppers, 164
Cranberry Gravy, Beef Brisket with, 13
Cranberry-Orange Pork Roast, 35, **35**
Creamy Beef Pitas, 138, **138**
Creamy Butternut Squash Soup, **106,**
    107
Creamy Wild Rice, 161
Crescent Dogs, 157
Cuban Black Bean Soup, 97
Curried Beef Stew, 112
Curry, Mango Chutney-Chicken, 57

Desserts
    Chocolate-Filled Crescents, 120
    Strawberry Shortcakes, 41
Dill-Turkey Chowder, 101
Double-Onion Beef Sandwiches, 134,
    134

Easy Barbecued Beef Sandwiches, 133
Easy Chicken Cacciatore, **70,** 71
Easy Pork Chop Suey, 38, **38**
Easy Scalloped Corn, 165
Enchilada Casserole, Ham and
    Chicken, 49

Family-Favorite Beef Stew, 114, **114**
Fish. *See* Seafood
Five-Spice Chicken Big Bowls, 69
French Onion Soup with Cheesy
    Bread, 108
Fruit Stuffing, Spiced, Pork Chops
    with, 39, **39**

garlic, jarred, buying, 134
Garlic Cheese Biscuits, 81
Garlic Herb Biscuits, 166
Garlic Smashed Red Potatoes, 168
Georgia-Style Barbecued Turkey
    Sandwiches, 150, **151**
Ginger Squash, 167, **167**
Gingered Pork Wraps, 140
gingerroot, storing, 38
Grandma's Chicken Noodle Soup,
    99, **99**
Greek Chicken Pita Folds, **146,** 147
Green Bean Casserole, Alfredo, 166,
    166
Ground Turkey and Beans, 87, **87**

Ham
    and Chicken Enchilada Casserole,
      49
    Cuban Black Bean Soup, 97
    'n' Cheese Biscuit Sandwiches, 105
    Sandwiches, Sweet-and-Saucy, 144
    Scalloped Potatoes, Tomatoes and,
      48
    Split Pea Soup with Veggies, 93
    Vegetable, and Bean Soup, 96

Hamburger-Noodle Soup, 98, **98**
Hearty Steak and Tater Soup, 95, **95**
Herbed Chicken and Stuffing Supper,
    56
Herbed Wild Rice Pilaf, 163, **163**
Home-Style Pork Stew, 110, **111**
Honey-Dijon Pork Roast, 33
Hot Beef Sandwiches au Jus, 132
Hot dogs
    Beans 'n Wieners, 53
    Corn Dogs, 158
    Crescent Dogs, 157
Hot Turkey Sandwiches, 148
Hungarian Stew, 113

Irish Stew, 116
Italian Biscuits, 45
Italian Ground Turkey Rolls, **130,** 152
Italian Sausage Lasagna, **46,** 47

Jambalaya with Red Beans and Rice,
    72
Jerked Chicken Hoagies, 145

Key West Ribs, 43, **43**

Lamb
    Dijon, 52
    Irish Stew, 116
    and Rice, Moroccan, 51, **51**
    Lasagna, Italian Sausage, **46,** 47
    lemon-pepper seasoning, home-
      made, 147
Lentil(s)
    BBQ Veggie Joes, 153
    types of, 124
    Vegetable and Pasta Stew, 124
Lumpy Cheese Bread, 95

Main dishes, meat. *See* Beef; Lamb;
    Pork
Main dishes, meatless. *See* Meatless
    Main Dishes
Main dishes, poultry. *See* Chicken;
    Turkey
Main dishes, seafood. *See* Seafood
Mango Chutney-Chicken Curry, 57
Meat. *See* Beef; Ham; Lamb; Pork;
    Sausage(s)
Meatless Main Dishes
    BBQ Veggie Joes, 153
    Couscous-Stuffed Peppers, 164
    Creamy Butternut Squash Soup,
      106, 107
    French Onion Soup with Cheesy
      Bread, 108
    Old-Fashioned Baked Beans, **154,**
      156
    Ratatouille Bean Stew, 125
    Savory Red Beans and Rice, 157
Meatless Main Dishes (*cont.*)
    Spicy Vegetarian Chili, 129

Tex-Mex Baked Beans, 158, **158**
Two-Potato Vegetable Soup, 105
Vegetable, Lentil and Pasta Stew, 124
Vegetable Minestrone Soup, 104
White Beans with Sun-Dried Tomatoes, 159, **159**
Winter Vegetable Stew, 122, **123**
Meaty Two-Bean Chili, 128
Mediterranean Steak Roll, 20
Mexicali Chicken and Corn Soup, 100
Mexican Round Steak, 16
Moroccan Chicken Stew, 120
Moroccan Lamb and Rice, 51, **51**
Mushrooms, Burgundy Beef and, 23, **23**

Old-Fashioned Baked Beans, **154**, 156
One-Pot Turkey Dinner, 86, **86**
Onion
    Au Gratin Potatoes and, 169
    Caramelized, Pot Roast, 14, **15**
    Double-, Beef Sandwiches, 134, **134**
    'n' Cream Crescents, 86
    Pepper Biscuits, Warm, 159
    Sauce, Herbed, Chicken Legs with, 77
    Soup, French, with Cheesy Bread, 108
Open-Faced Pizza Sandwiches, 143, **143**

Parmesan Rosemary Crescents, 79
parsnips, about, 122
Pasta
    Cheesy Italian Tortellini, 31, **31**
    Chicken Fettuccine Alfredo, 60
    Italian Sausage Lasagna, **46**, 47
    Ravioli with Smoked Sausage and Peppers, 45
    Sauce, Bolognese, with Spaghetti, 44
    Turkey-Rotini Casserole, 83, **83**
    Vegetable, and Lentil Stew, 124
Pea, Split, Soup with Veggies, 93
Pea, Yellow, Soup with Chorizo, 94, **94**
Peachy Glazed Sweet Potatoes, 171, **171**
Peanut Chicken, Thai, 65
Peas, Black-Eyed, Spicy, 160
Peppers, Couscous-Stuffed, 164
Peppers, Ravioli with Smoked Sausage and, 45
Peppery Fish Chowder, 103, **103**
Philly Cheese Steak Sandwiches, 135, **135**
Picadillo with Apples and Almonds, 29
Pie, Pot, Chicken Stroganoff, 66, **66**
Pie, Tamale, Beef and Bean, 26, **27**
Pilaf, Herbed Wild Rice, 163, **163**

Pilaf, Vegetable-Rice, 162, **162**
Pineapple
    Chicken Drumsticks with Sweet Potatoes and, 75, **75**
    and Pork, 37
    Sweet-and-Saucy Ham Sandwiches, 144
    Sweet-and-Sour Chicken with Rice, **54**, 76
Pizza Pork Chops, 40
Pizza Sandwiches, Open-Faced, 143, **143**
plum sauce, about, 89
Polenta, Beef Ragout on, 22, **22**
Pork. See also Ham; Sausage(s)
    and Beef Chili, Chunky, 127, **127**
    and Cabbage Soup, 92
    Chop Suey, Easy, 38, **38**
    Chops, Pizza, 40
    Chops with Spiced Fruit Stuffing, 39, **39**
    Key West Ribs, 43, **43**
    and Pineapple, 37
    Porketta with Two Potatoes, 34, **34**
    pulled, leftover, storing, 142
    Pulled-, Burritos, 142, **142**
    ribs, about, 42
    Ribs with Molasses-Mustard Sauce, 41
    Roast, Cranberry-Orange, 35, **35**
    Roast, Honey-Dijon, 33
    Roast Dinner, Autumn, 36
    Slow-and-Easy Barbecued Ribs, 42, **42**
    Split Pea Soup with Veggies, 93
    Stew, Home-Style, 110, **111**
    Wraps, Gingered, 140
Porketta with Two Potatoes, 34, **34**
Pot Pie, Chicken Stroganoff, 66, **66**
Potato(es)
    Chile-Cheese Party, 170, **170**
    hash browns, buying, 170
    Hearty Steak and Tater Soup, 95, **95**
    and Onion, Au Gratin, 169
    Red, Garlic Smashed, 168
    Scalloped, Tomatoes, and Ham, 48
    Two, Porketta with, 34, **34**
    Two-, Vegetable Soup, 105
Poultry. See Chicken; Turkey
Pretzels, Soft, 53
Pulled-Pork Burritos, 142, **142**

Ratatouille Bean Stew, 125
Ravioli with Smoked Sausage and Peppers, 45
Rice. See also Wild Rice
    converted, about, 162
    Jambalaya with Red Beans and, 72
    Moroccan Lamb and, 51, **51**
    Pilaf, Vegetable-, 162, **162**
    Savory Red Beans and, 157

Sweet-and-Sour Chicken with, **54**, 76
Rosemary Beef and Tomatoes, 25

Salsa Chicken, 67, **67**
Sandwiches
    BBQ Veggie Joes, 153
    Bratwurst and Sauerkraut, 141
    Cheeseburger, 139, **139**
    Corn Dogs, 158
    Creamy Beef Pitas, 138, **138**
    Crescent Dogs, 157
    Double-Onion Beef, 134, **134**
    Easy Barbecued Beef, 133
    Georgia-Style Barbecued Turkey, 150, **151**
    Gingered Pork Wraps, 140
    Greek Chicken Pita Folds, **146**, 147
    Ham 'n' Cheese Biscuit, 105
    Hot Beef, au Jus, 132
    Hot Turkey, 148
    Italian Ground Turkey Rolls, **130**, 152
    Jerked Chicken Hoagies, 145
    Open-Faced Pizza, 143, **143**
    Philly Cheese Steak, 135, **135**
    Pulled-Pork Burritos, 142, **142**
    Sloppy Joe Shortcakes, 137
    So-Easy Sloppy Joes, 137
    Southwest Beef, 136
    Sweet-and-Saucy Ham, 144
    Tex-Mex Wraps with Turkey, 149
Saucy Pepper Steak, **10**, 17
Sauerbraten, 24
Sauerkraut, Bratwurst and, 141
Sausage(s)
    Bolognese Pasta Sauce with Spaghetti, 44
    Bratwurst and Sauerkraut, 141
    Cheesy Italian Tortellini, 31, **31**
    Chicken, and Cabbage Stew with Wild Rice, 117
    chorizo, about, 94
    Italian, Lasagna, **46**, 47
    Jambalaya with Red Beans and Rice, 72
    Meaty Two-Bean Chili, 128
    Open-Faced Pizza Sandwiches, 143, **143**
    Smoked, and Peppers, Ravioli with, 45
    and Winter Root Casserole, 50, **50**
    Yellow Pea Soup with Chorizo, 94, **94**
Savory Red Beans and Rice, 157
Savory Turkey Breast, 78, **78**
Scalloped Potatoes, Tomatoes and Ham, 48
Seafood
    Jambalaya with Red Beans and Rice, 72

Peppery Fish Chowder, 103, **103**
Stew, **118,** 119
Side Dishes. **See also** Breads
  Alfredo Green Bean Casserole,
    166, **166**
  Au Gratin Potatoes and Onion,
    169
  Chile-Cheese Party Potatoes, 170,
    170
  Couscous-Stuffed Peppers, 164
  Creamy Wild Rice, 161
  Easy Scalloped Corn, 165
  Garlic Smashed Red Potatoes, 168
  Ginger Squash, 167, **167**
  Herbed Wild Rice Pilaf, 163, **163**
  Old-Fashioned Baked Beans, **154,**
    156
  Peachy Glazed Sweet Potatoes,
    171, **171**
  Savory Red Beans and Rice, 157
  Spicy Black-Eyed Peas, 160
  Tex-Mex Baked Beans, 158, **158**
  Vegetable-Rice Pilaf, 162, **162**
  White Beans with Sun-Dried
    Tomatoes, 159, **159**
Sloppy Joe Shortcakes, 137
Sloppy Joes, So-Easy, 137
Slow-and-Easy Barbecued Ribs, 42,
    42
slow cookers
  high altitude adjustments, 9
  strategies and tips for, 6–9
  types and sizes of, 6
Smothered Buttermilk Chicken over
    Biscuits, 74, **74**
So-Easy Sloppy Joes, 137
Soft Pretzels, 53
Soup
  Cabbage and Pork, 92
  Creamy Butternut Squash, **106,**
    107
  Cuban Black Bean, 97
  Dill-Turkey Chowder, 101
  French Onion, with Cheesy Bread,
    108
  Grandma's Chicken Noodle, 99,
    99
  Hamburger-Noodle, 98, **98**
  Hearty Steak and Tater, 95, **95**
  Mexicali Chicken and Corn, 100
  Peppery Fish Chowder, 103, **103**
  Split Pea, with Veggies, 93
  Turkey-Wild Rice, 102, **102**
  Two-Potato Vegetable, 105
  Vegetable, Bean and Ham, 96
  Vegetable Minestrone, 104
  Yellow Pea, with Chorizo, 94, **94**
Southwest Beef Sandwiches, 136
Southwestern Chicken and Bean
    Stew, 115, **115**
Southwestern Turkey, 88
Spanish Chicken, 63, **63**

Spicy Black-Eyed Peas, 160
Spicy Vegetarian Chili, 129
Split Pea Soup with Veggies, 93
Squash, Butternut, Soup, Creamy,
    106, 107
Squash, Ginger, 167, **167**
Stew. See also Chili
  Chicken, Sausage and Cabbage,
    with Wild Rice, 117
  Chicken Brunswick, 121
  Curried Beef, 112
  Family-Favorite Beef, 114, **114**
  Home-Style Pork, 110, **111**
  Hungarian, 113
  Irish, 116
  Moroccan Chicken, 120
  Ratatouille Bean, 125
  Seafood, **118,** 119
  Southwestern Chicken and Bean,
    115, **115**
  Swiss Steak, 109
  Vegetable, Lentil and Pasta, 124
  Winter Vegetable, 122, **123**
Strawberry Shortcakes, 41
Stuffing, Spiced Fruit, Pork Chops
    with, 39, **39**
Stuffing, Turkey and, with Onion
    Glaze, 81
Sweet-and-Saucy Ham Sandwiches,
    144
Sweet-and-Sour Chicken with Rice,
    54, 76
Sweet Potatoes
  Peachy Glazed, 171, **171**
  and Pineapple, Chicken
    Drumsticks with, 75, **75**
  Porketta with Two Potatoes, 34, **34**
  Two-Potato Vegetable Soup, 105
Swiss Steak Stew, 109
Swiss Steak Supper, 21

Tamale Pie, Beef and Bean, 26, **27**
Tex-Mex Baked Beans, 158, **158**
Tex-Mex Wraps with Turkey, 149
Texas Chili, **90,** 126, **126**
Thai Peanut Chicken, 65
Tomatoes
  Bolognese Pasta Sauce with
    Spaghetti, 44
  Cajun Pot Roast with Corn and, 12
  Rosemary Beef and, 25
  Scalloped Potatoes, Ham and, 48
  Sun-Dried, White Beans with, 159,
    159
Tortilla(s)
  Casserole, Beefy, 30, **30**
  Gingered Pork Wraps, 140
  Ham and Chicken Enchilada
    Casserole, 49
  Pulled-Pork Burritos, 142, **142**
  Tex-Mex Wraps with Turkey,
    149

Turkey
  -Dill Chowder, 101
  -Rotini Casserole, 83, **83**
  -Wild Rice Soup, 102, **102**
  and Bacon Wild Rice Casserole,
    79, **79**
  and Bean Cassoulet, 84
  Breast, Savory, 78, **78**
  breast, thawing, 80
  Breast with Bulgur and Feta
    Cheese, 80
  with Cornmeal-Thyme Dumplings,
    85
  Dinner, One-Pot, 86, **86**
  Drumsticks with Plum Sauce, 89
  Ground, and Beans, 87, **87**
  Ground, Rolls, Italian, **130,** 152
  Sandwiches, Georgia-Style
    Barbecued, 150, **151**
  Sandwiches, Hot, 148
  Southwestern, 88
  and Stuffing with Onion Glaze, 81
  Tex-Mex Wraps with, 149
  and Vegetables, Barbecued, 82, **82**
Two-Potato Vegetable Soup, 105

Veal Paprika, 32
Vegetable(s). **See also specific**
    vegetables
  -Rice Pilaf, 162, **162**
  Barbecued Turkey and, 82, **82**
  BBQ Veggie Joes, 153
  Bean and Ham Soup, 96
  Easy Pork Chop Suey, 38, **38**
  Lentil, and Pasta Stew, 124
  Minestrone Soup, 104
  One-Pot Turkey Dinner, 86, **86**
  Soup, Two-Potato, 105
  Split Pea Soup with Veggies, 93
  Winter, Stew, 122, **123**
  Winter Root and Sausage
    Casserole, 50, **50**
Vegetarian Chili, Spicy, 129

Warm Onion Pepper Biscuits, 159
White Beans with Sun-Dried
    Tomatoes, 159, **159**
Wild Rice
  -Turkey Soup, 102, **102**
  Casserole, Turkey and Bacon, 79,
    79
  Chicken, Sausage and Cabbage
    Stew with, 117
  Creamy, 161
  Pilaf, Herbed, 163, **163**
  washing, 163
Winter Root and Sausage Casserole,
    50, **50**
Winter Vegetable Stew, 122, **123**

Yellow Pea Soup with Chorizo, 94,
    94

Titles by Pillsbury

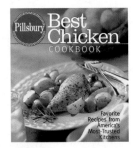

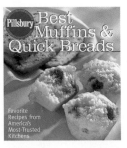

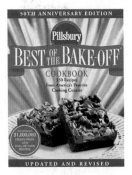

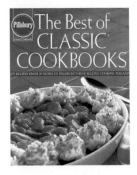

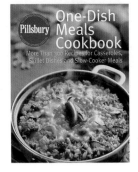

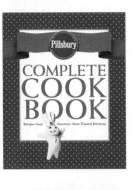

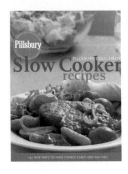